Drawn & colored by Velvet Comeau

Drawn & colored by Johanna Ans

Global Doodle Gems Volume 13
"The Ultimate international Coloring Book...an Epic Collection from Artists around the World!"

Drawn & colored by Peggy Sue's art

Drawn & colored by Small Fish

Drawn by Yaya & colored by Cressam

Drawn & colored by Creative Rosalien

Drawn & colored by Angel Huang

Drawn & colored by Adriana Graciela Volpe

Drawn & colored by Audrey Sagh

Drawn by Ahmed Fouad & colored by Vero Pignot

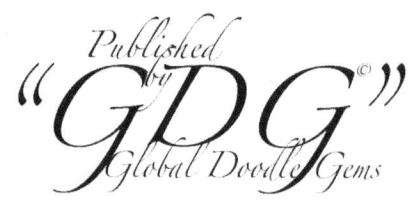

Share your colored versions with us ! We love seeing your results and hearing from you we are social !

The Official FB book page, stay on top of what we have in the works !
www.facebook.com/globaldoodlegems

The Community group, share your colored pages, meet the artists, enjoy exclusive freebies, take part in community Charity books and so much more......
www.facebook.com/groups/globaldoodlegems/

Follow us on Twitter.... @GlobalDoodlegem

We are on Instagram too
@globaldoodlegems for instagram

...and if you are not social like that we have a blog
globaldoodlegems.wordpress.com

Copyright © 2016 Global Doodle Gems

All rights are reserved by Global Doodle Gems.

Duplication of pages for personal use are allowed. You are invited to color the pages then scan/post your coloured versions to social networks, mentioning the book title and author/artist (Global Doodle Gems).

All artwork and images are protected by copyright laws. This book or any portion thereof may not, otherwise, be reproduced and/or distributed or transmitted without the express written permission of the artist/publisher of Global Doodle Gems.

All of us from the Global Doodle Gems wish you a colortastic time and look forward to seeing your wonderful color results online !

Chapter 1
Velvet Comeau

Chapter 2
MWMS Johanna Ans

Chapter 3
Wenyu Lin Small Fish

Chapter 4
Peggy Sue's Artwork

Chapter 5
Yaya

Chapter 6
Creative Rosalien

Chapter 7
Adriana Graciela Volpe

Chapter 8
Angel Huang

Chapter 9
Audrey Sagh

Chapter 10
Ahmed Fouad

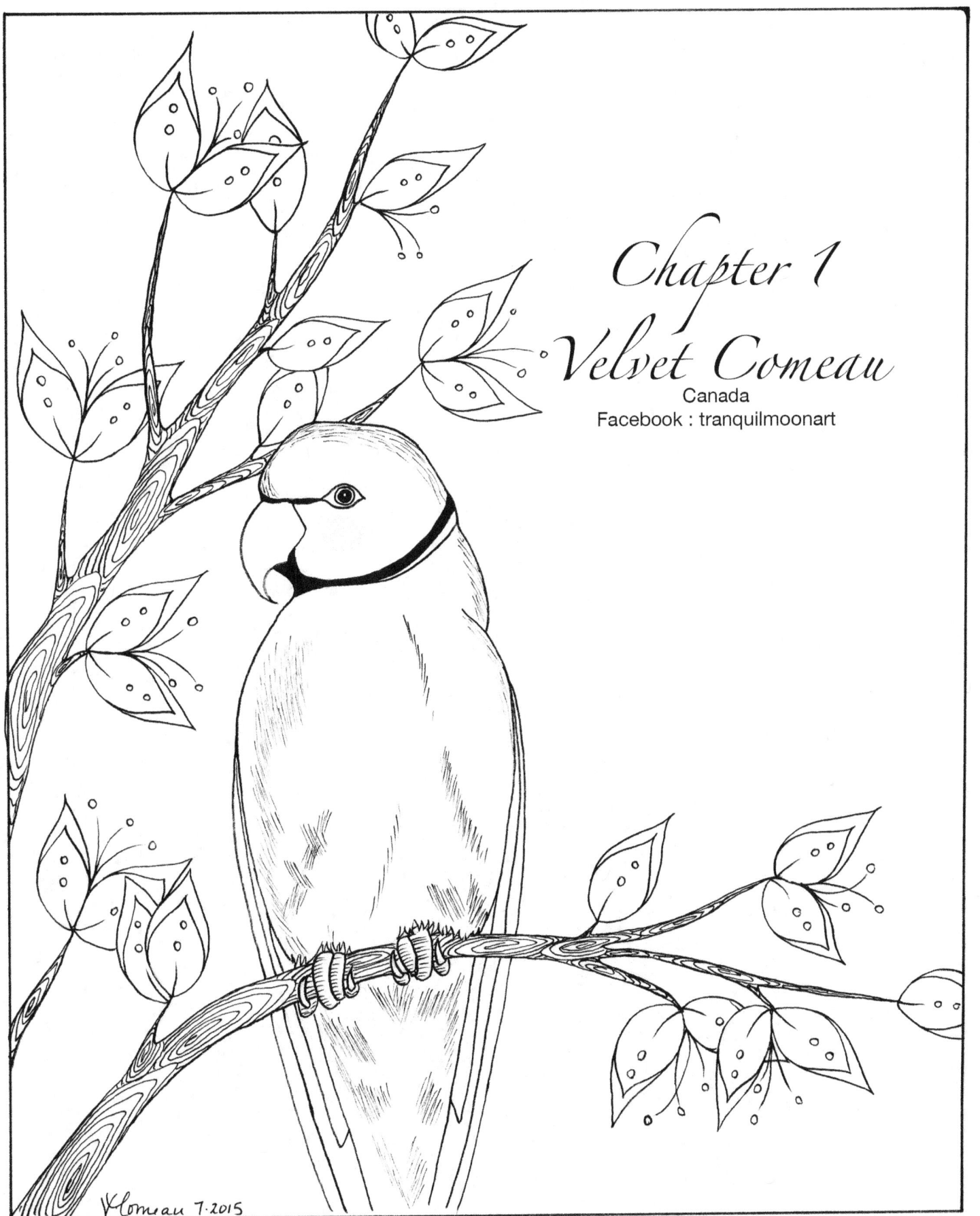

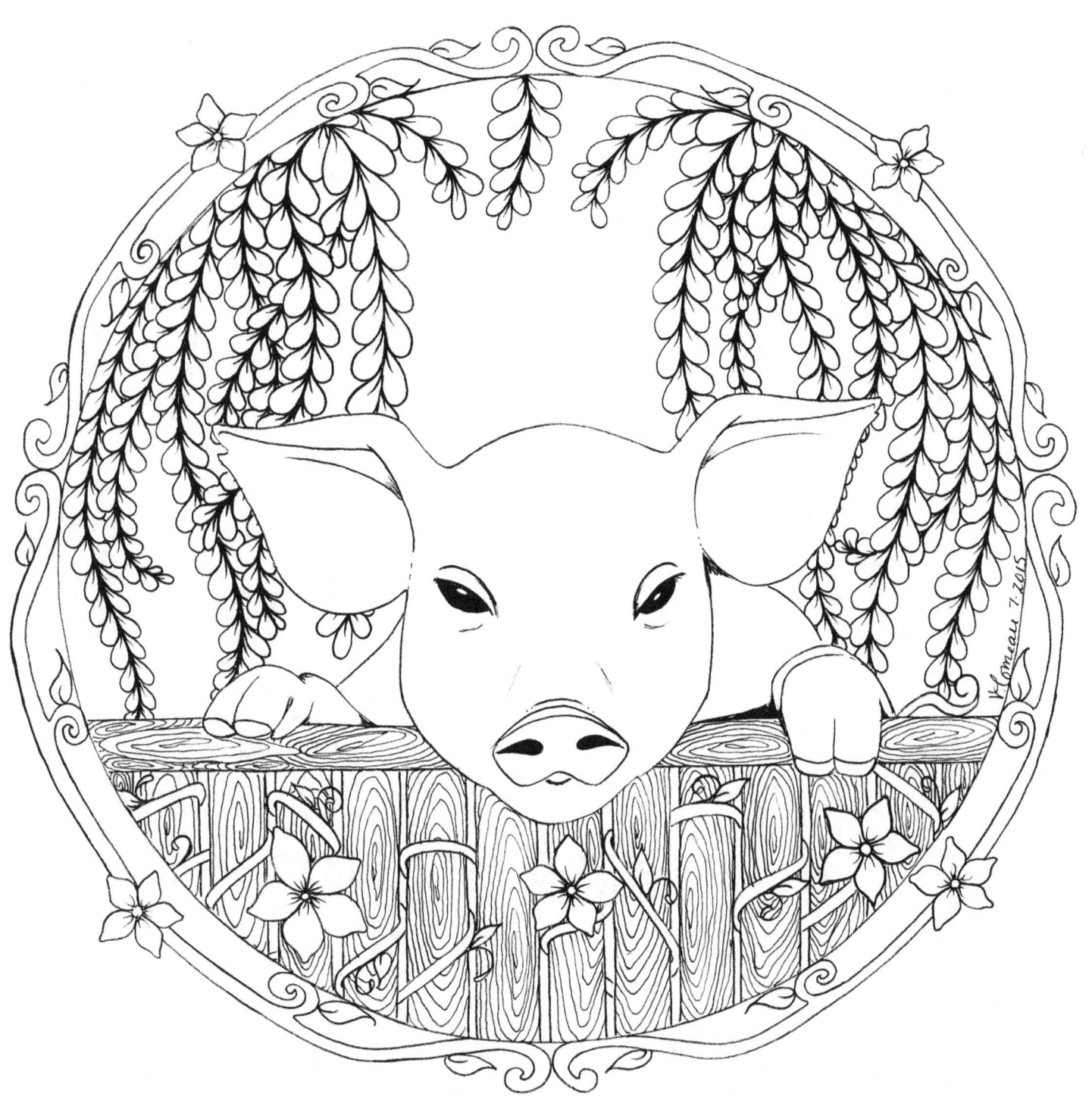

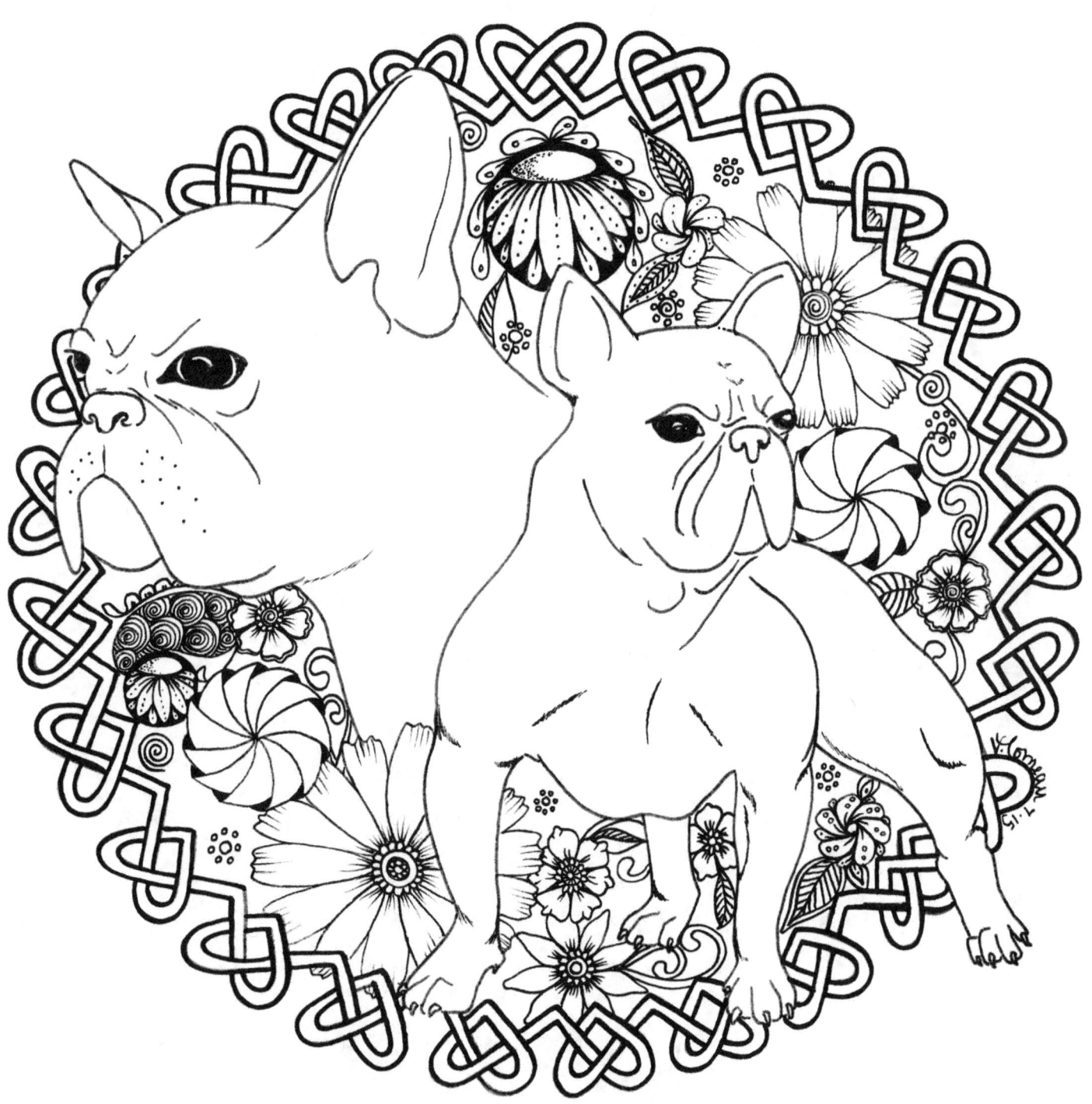

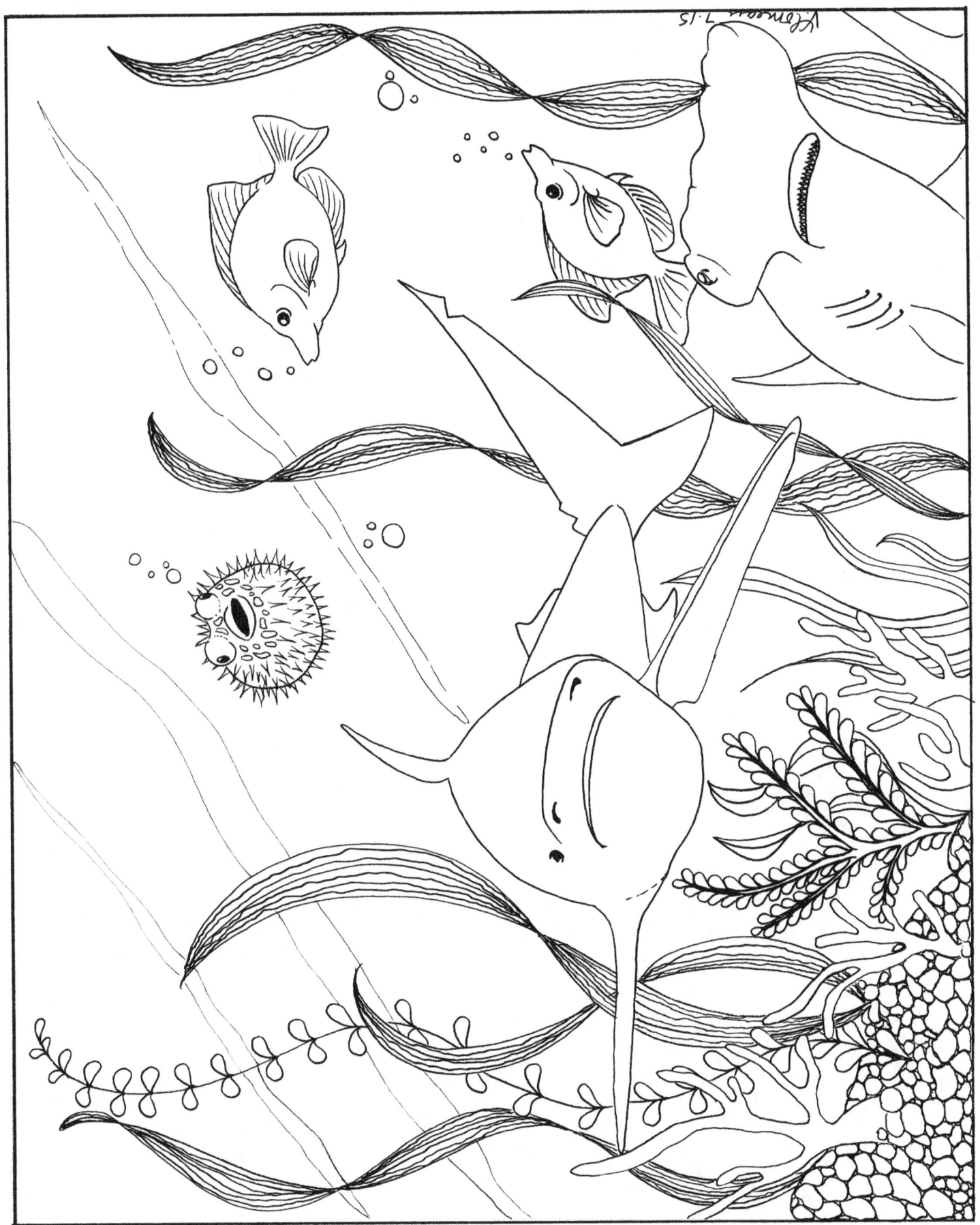

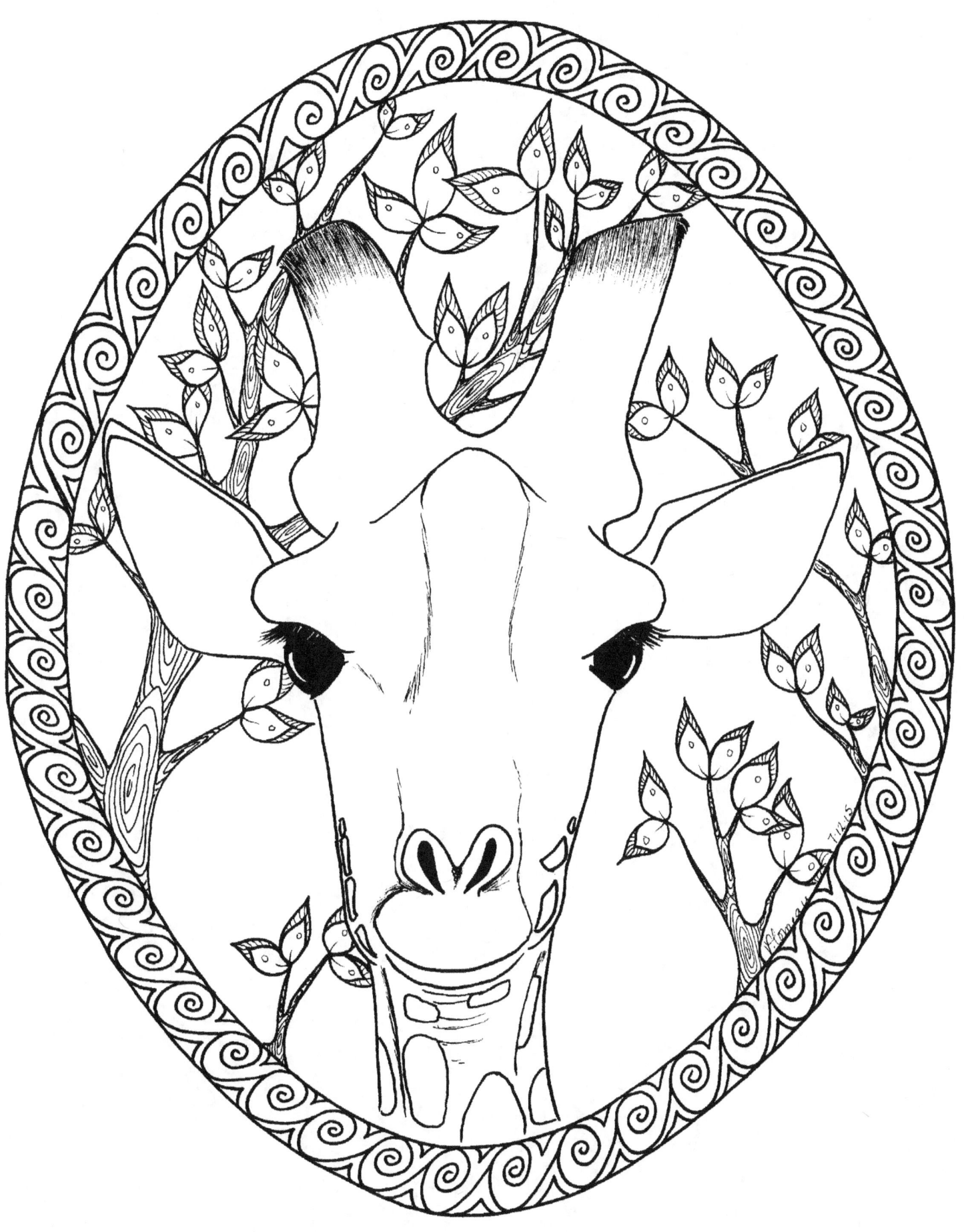

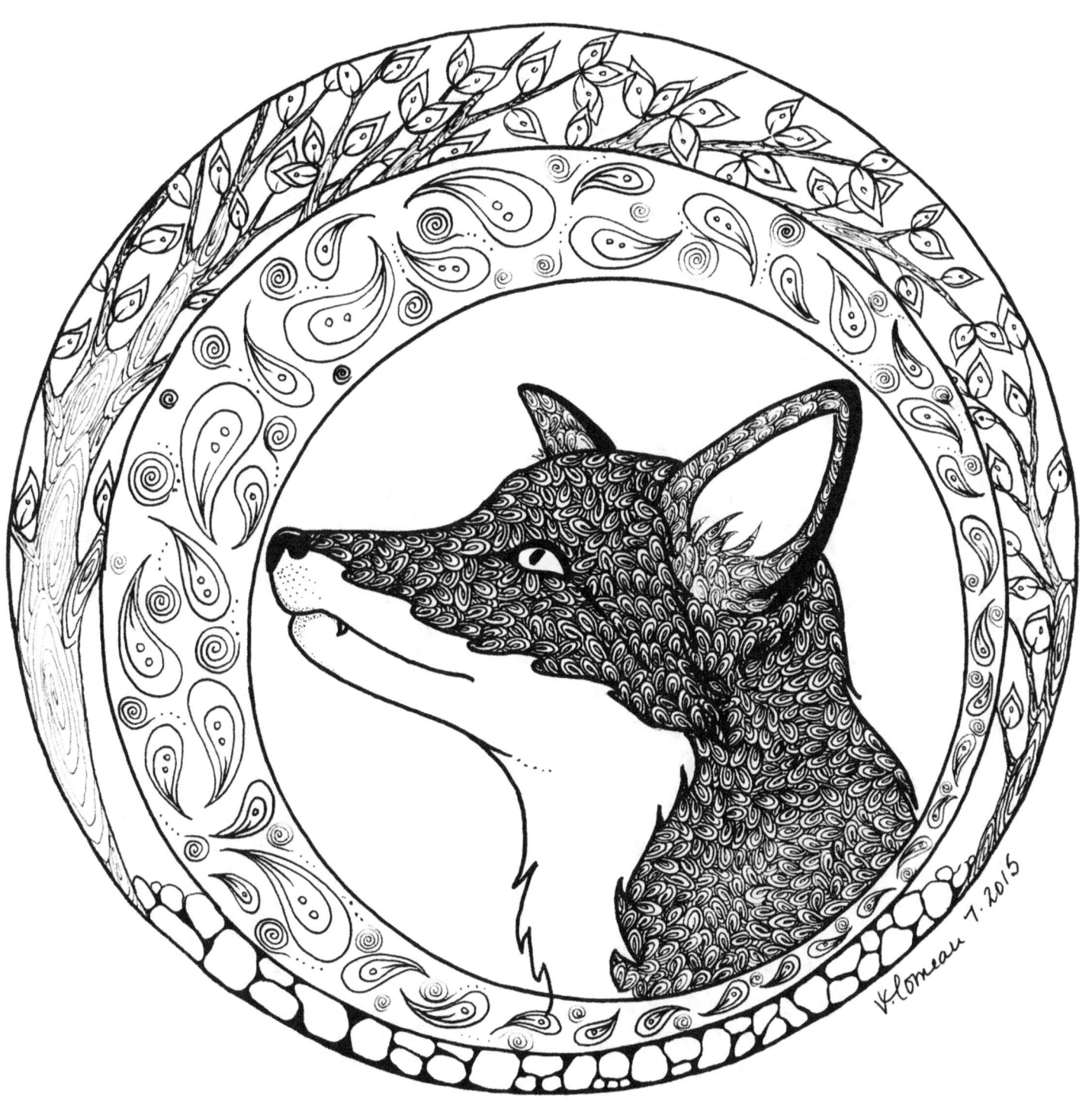

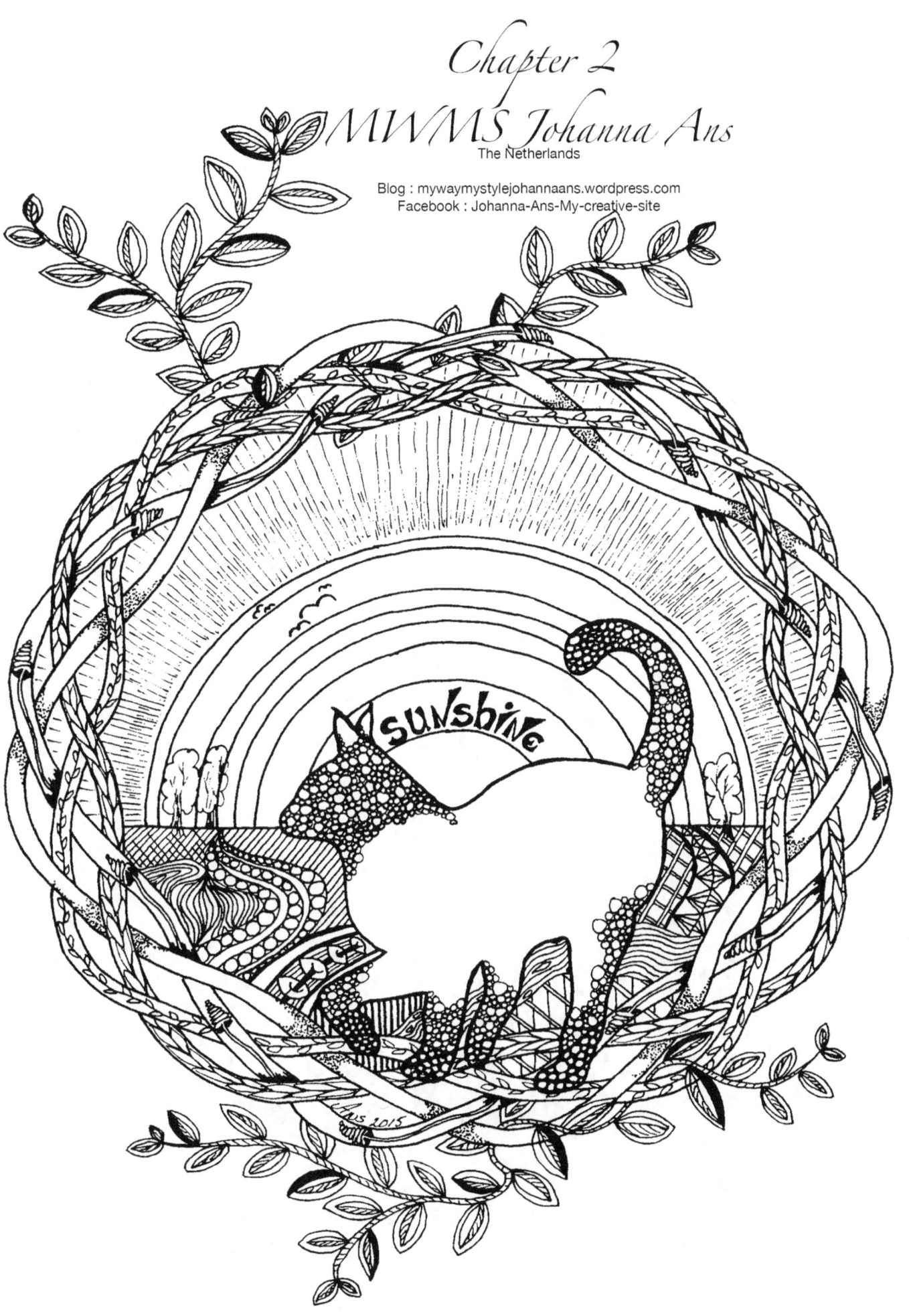

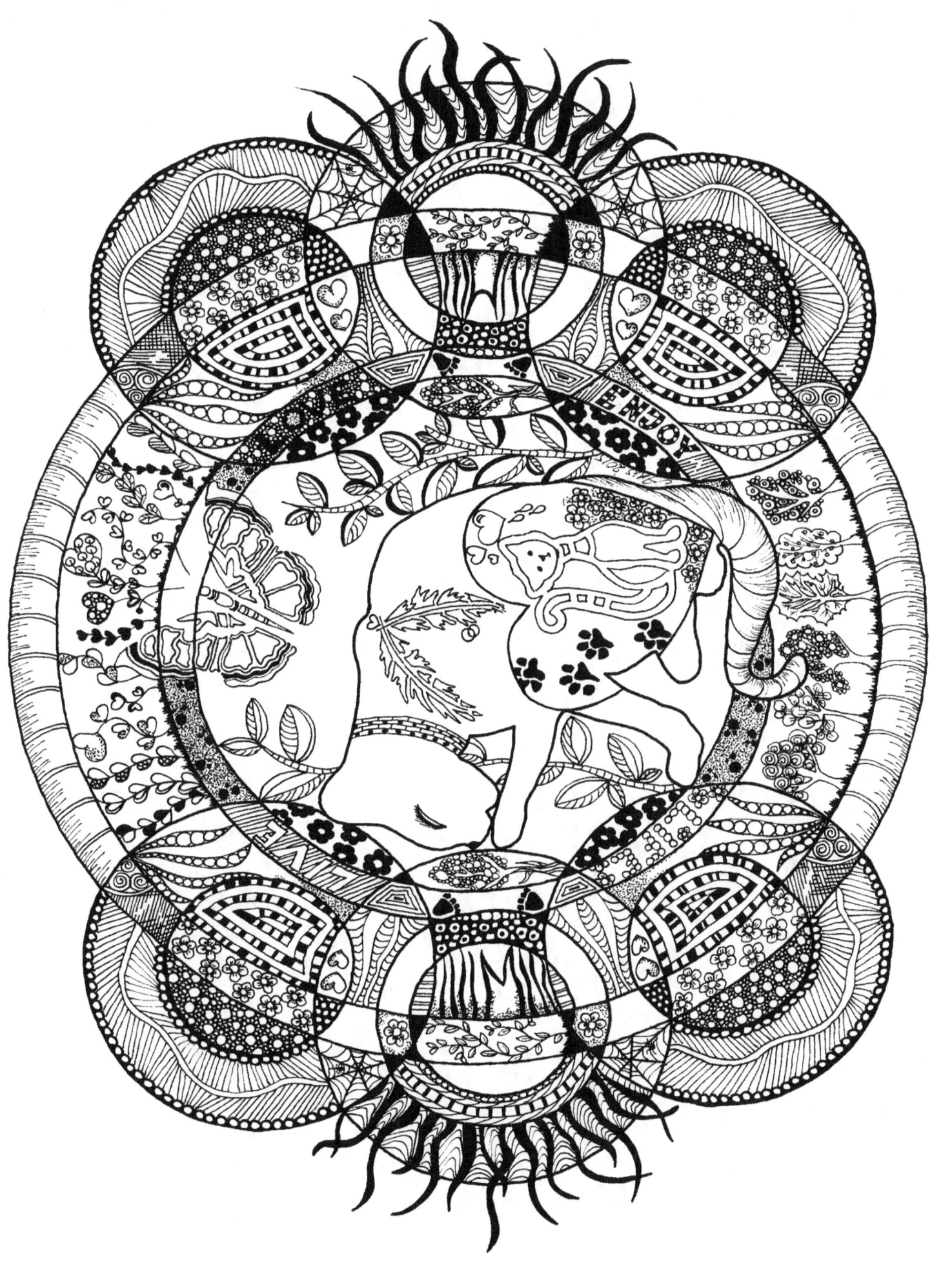

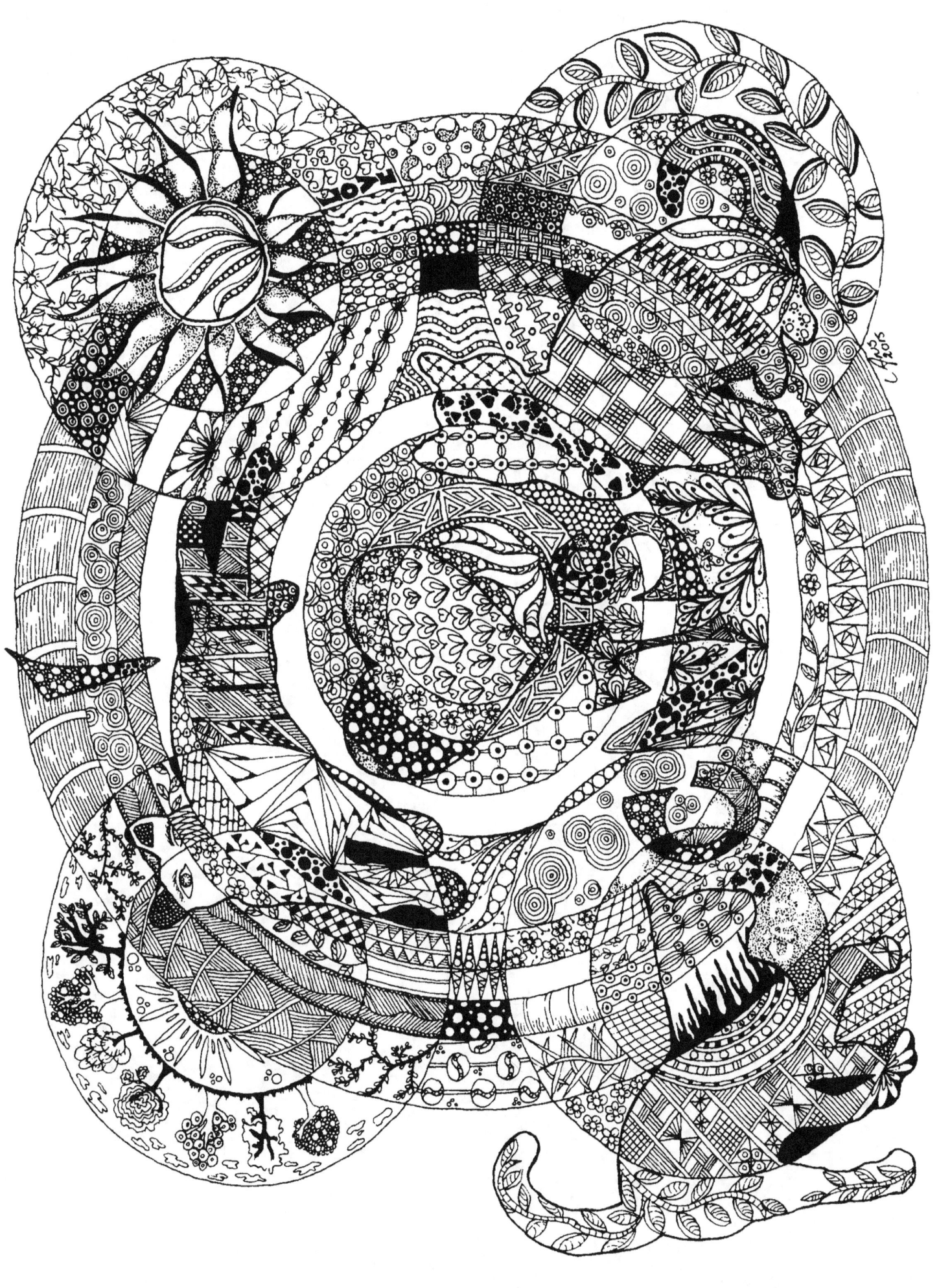

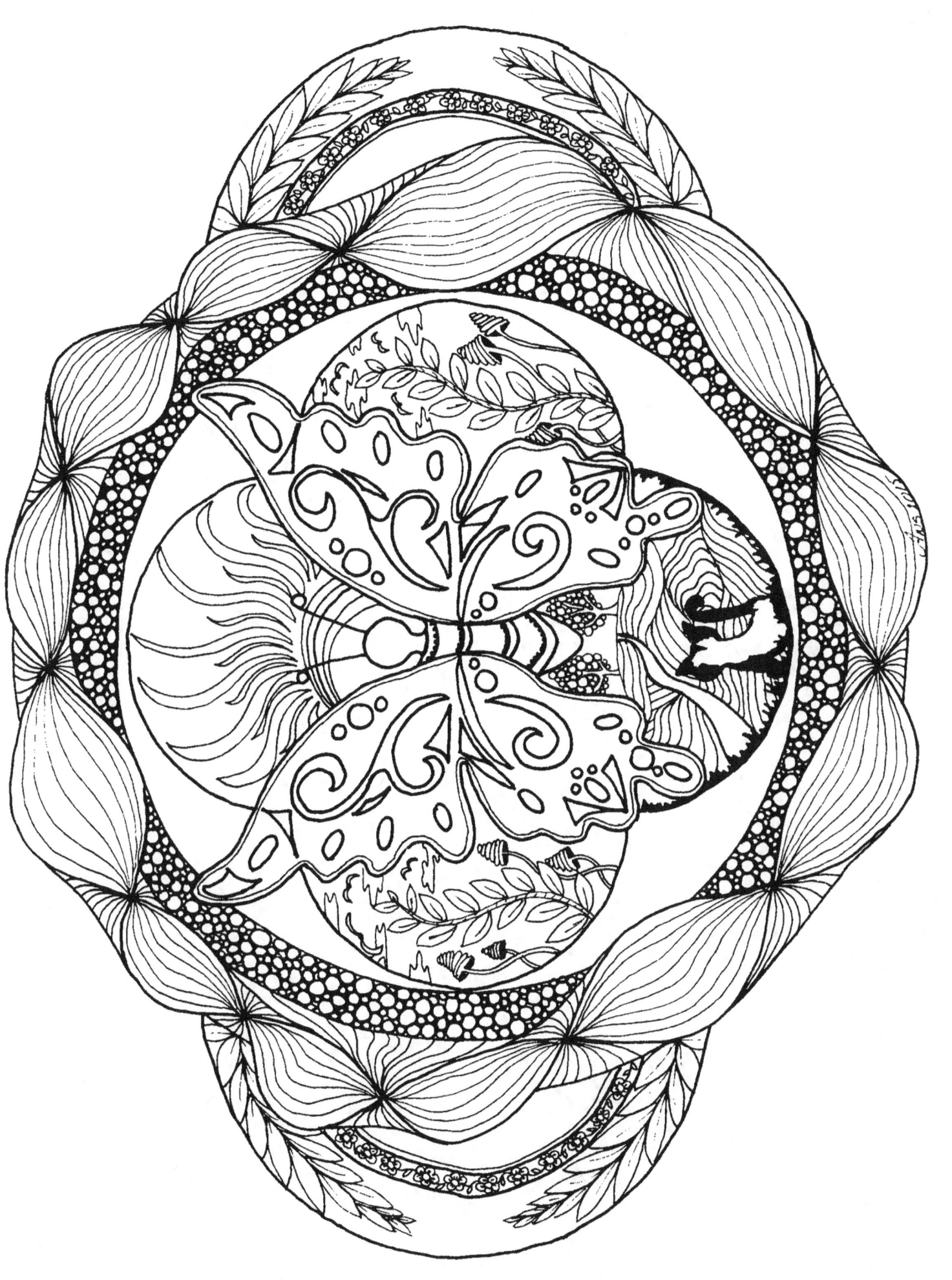

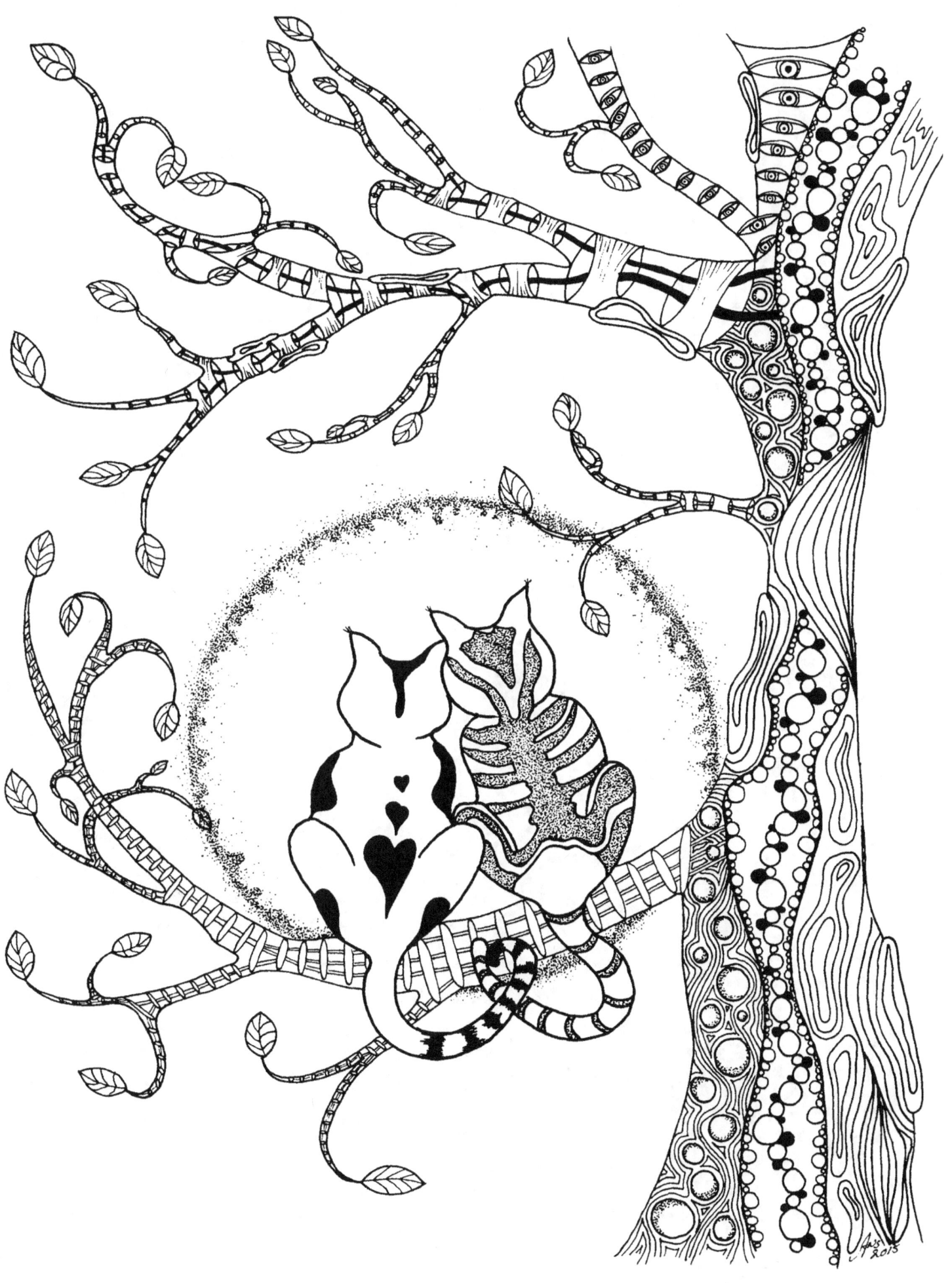

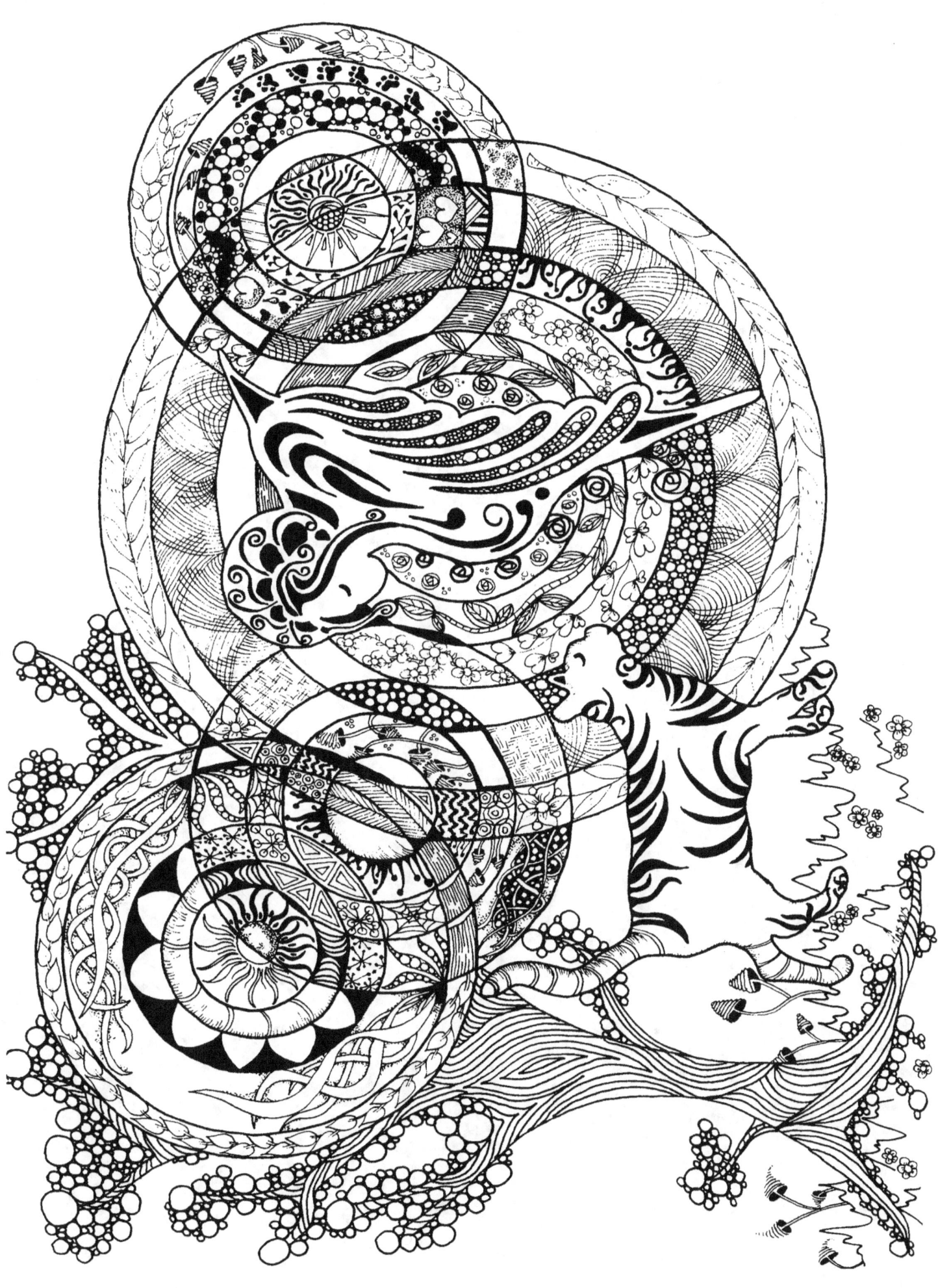

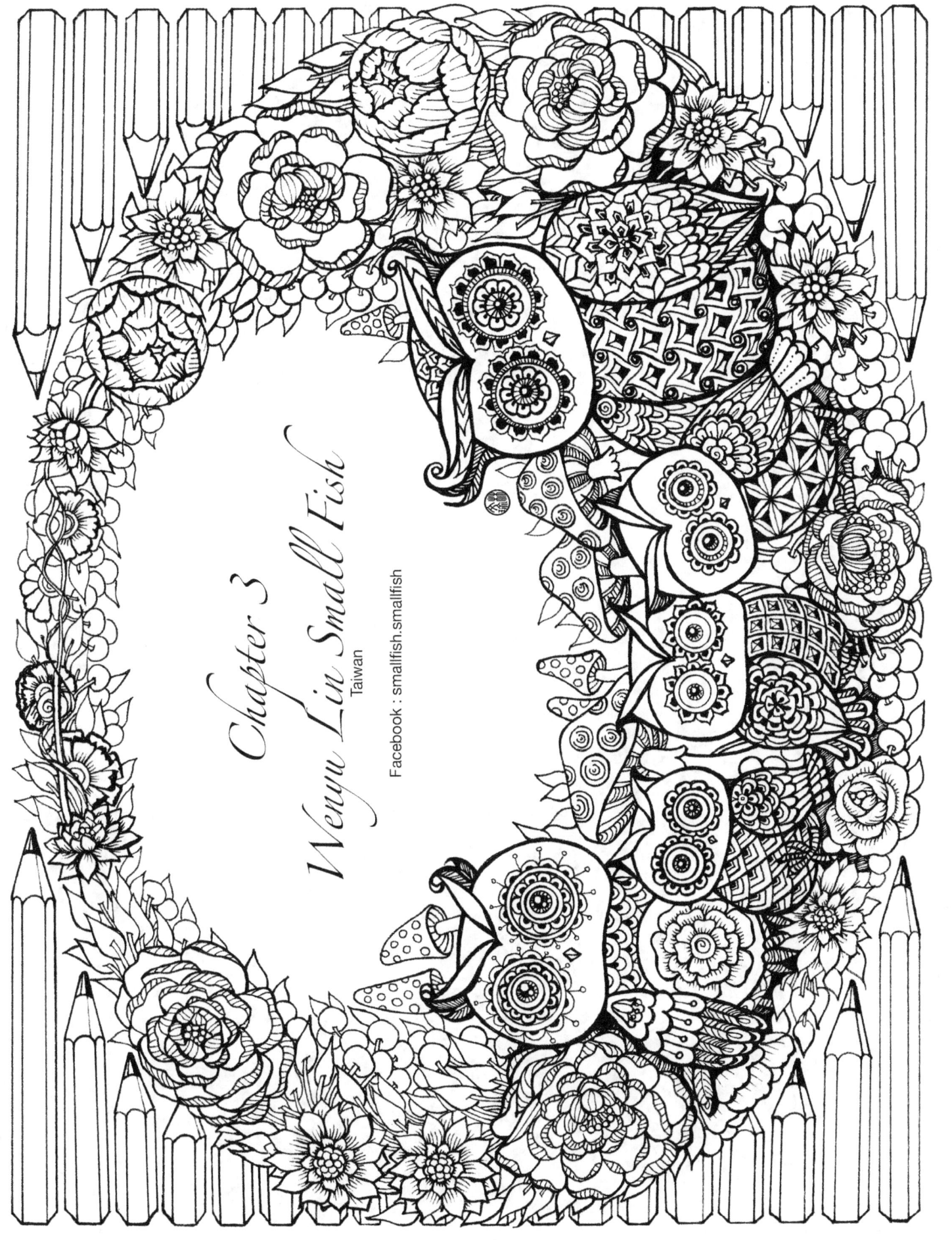

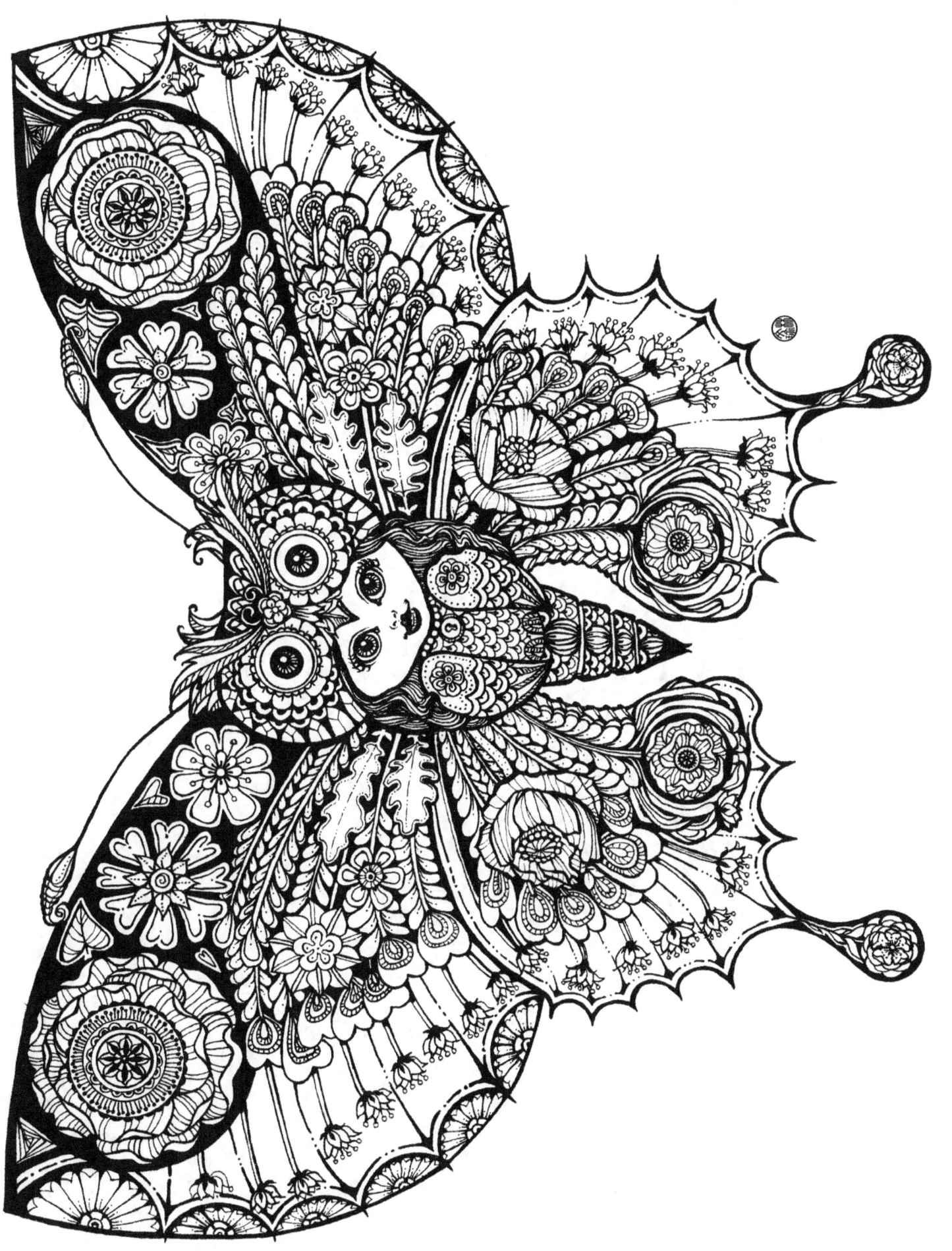

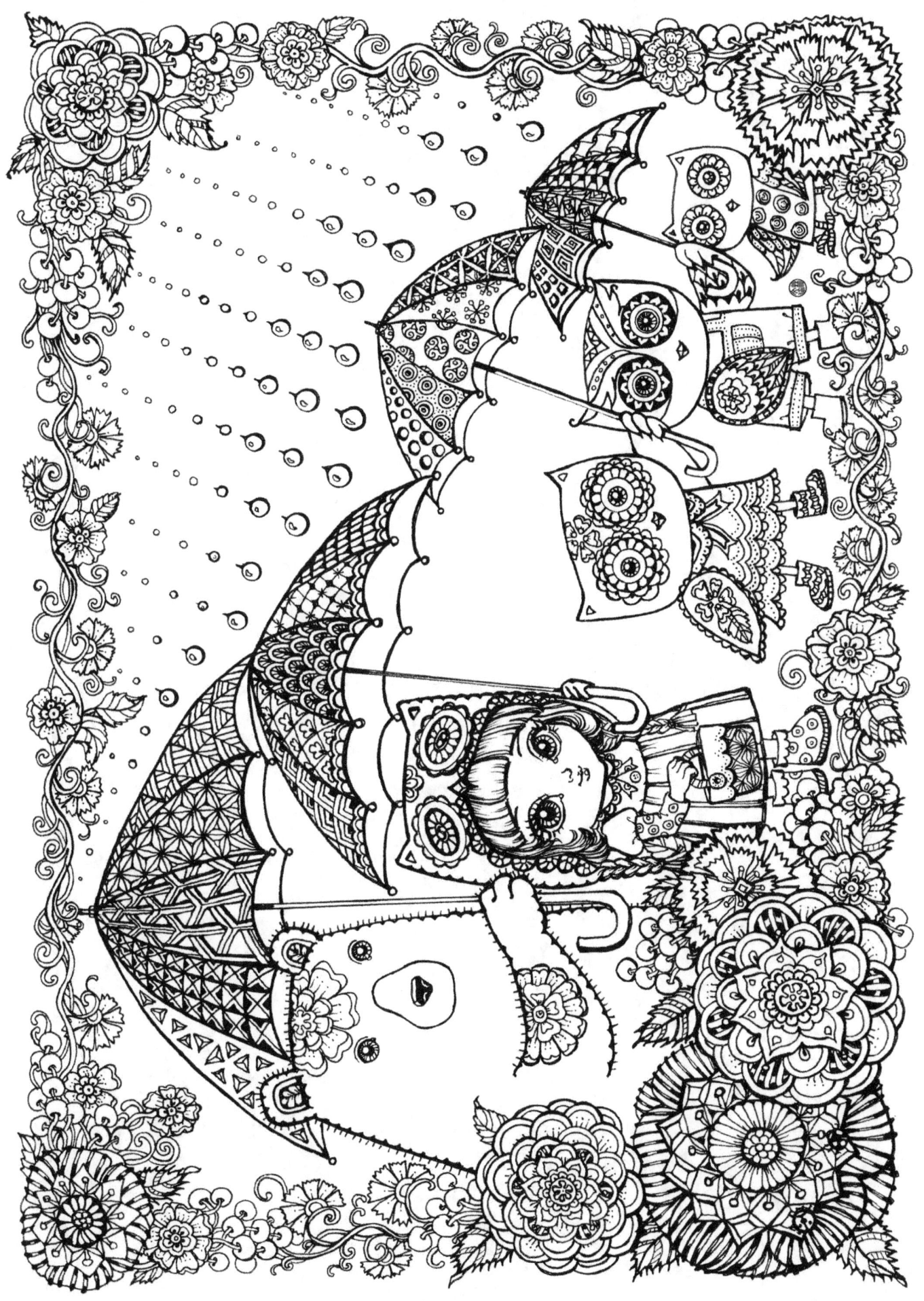

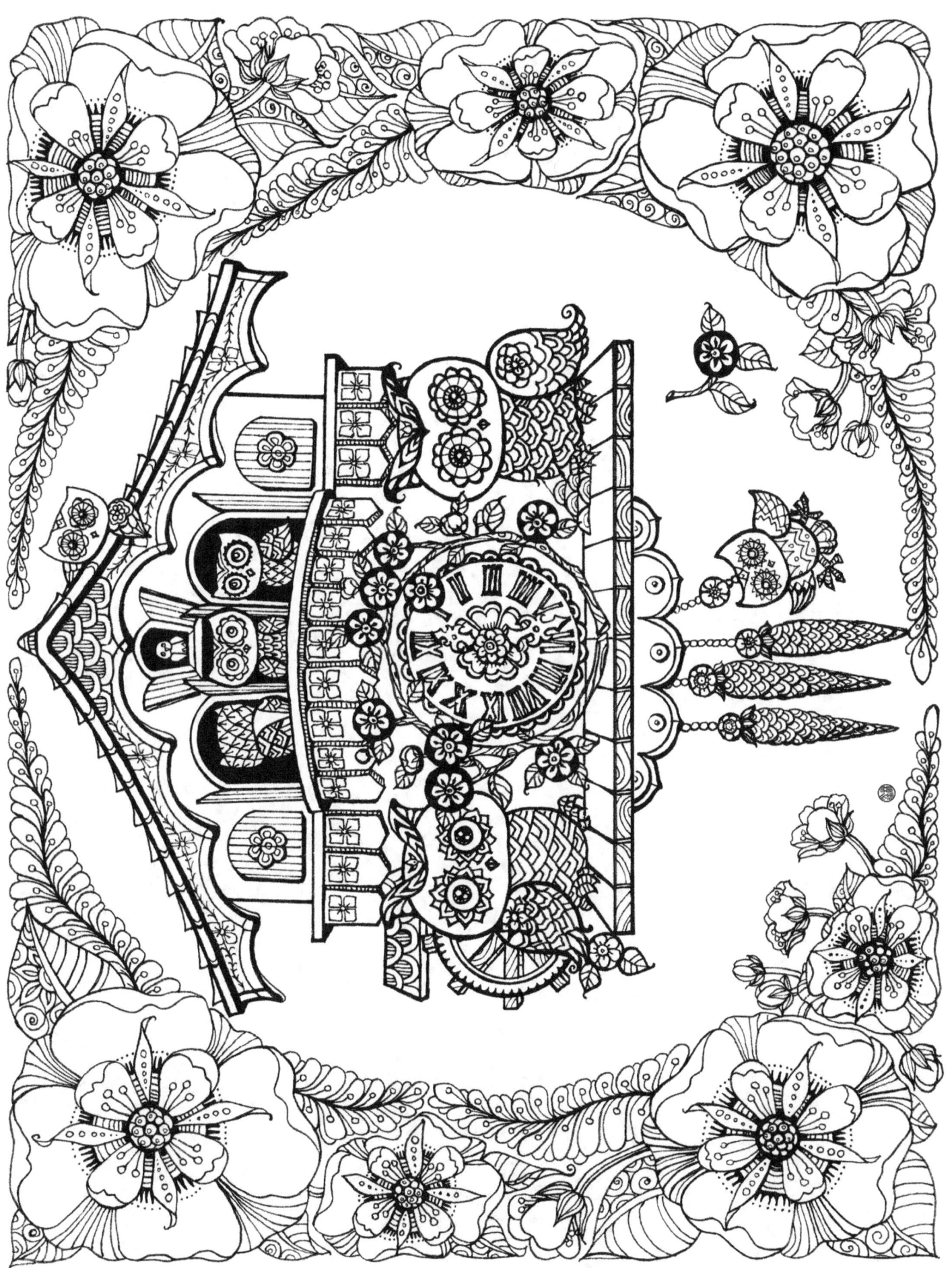

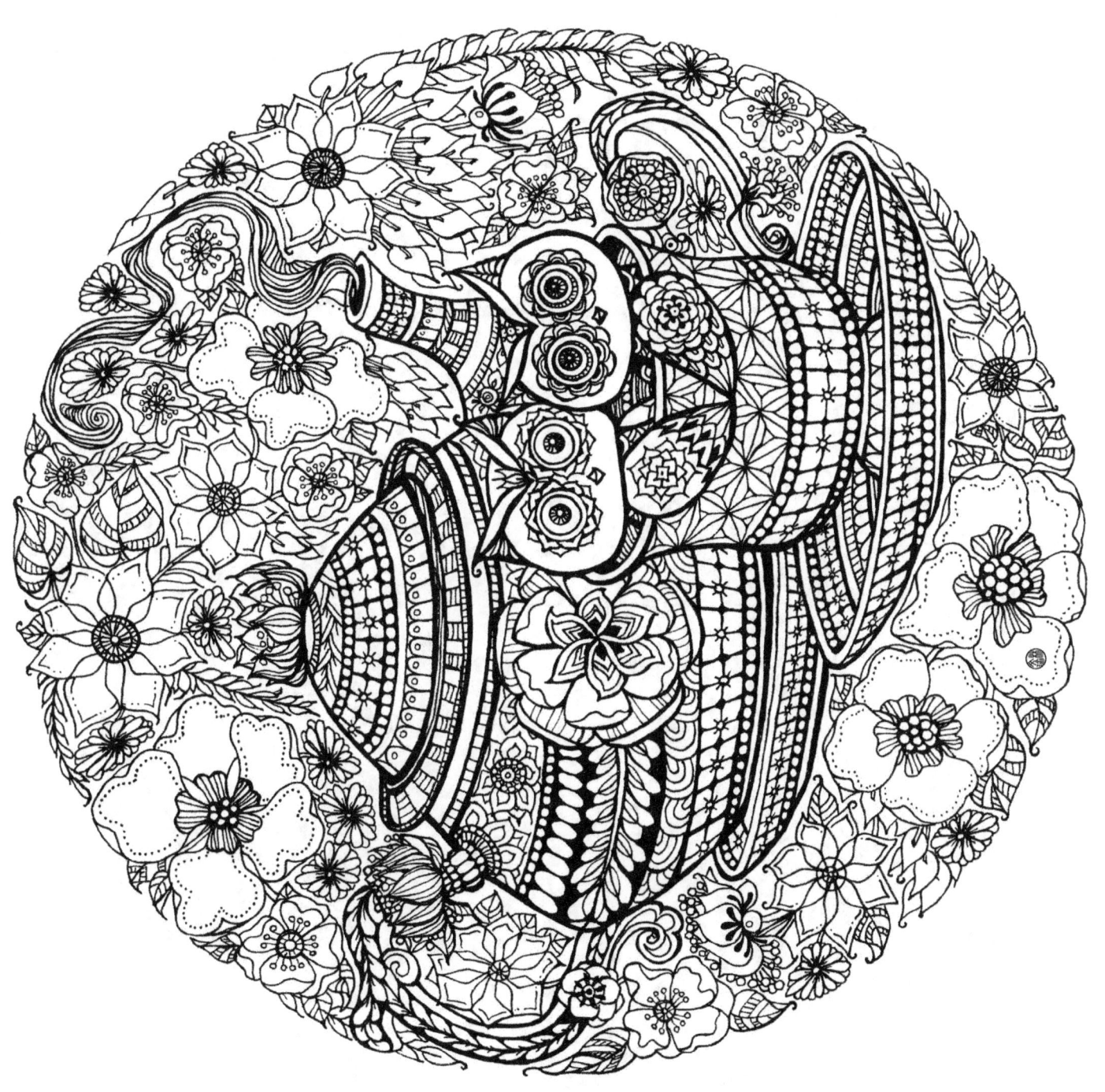

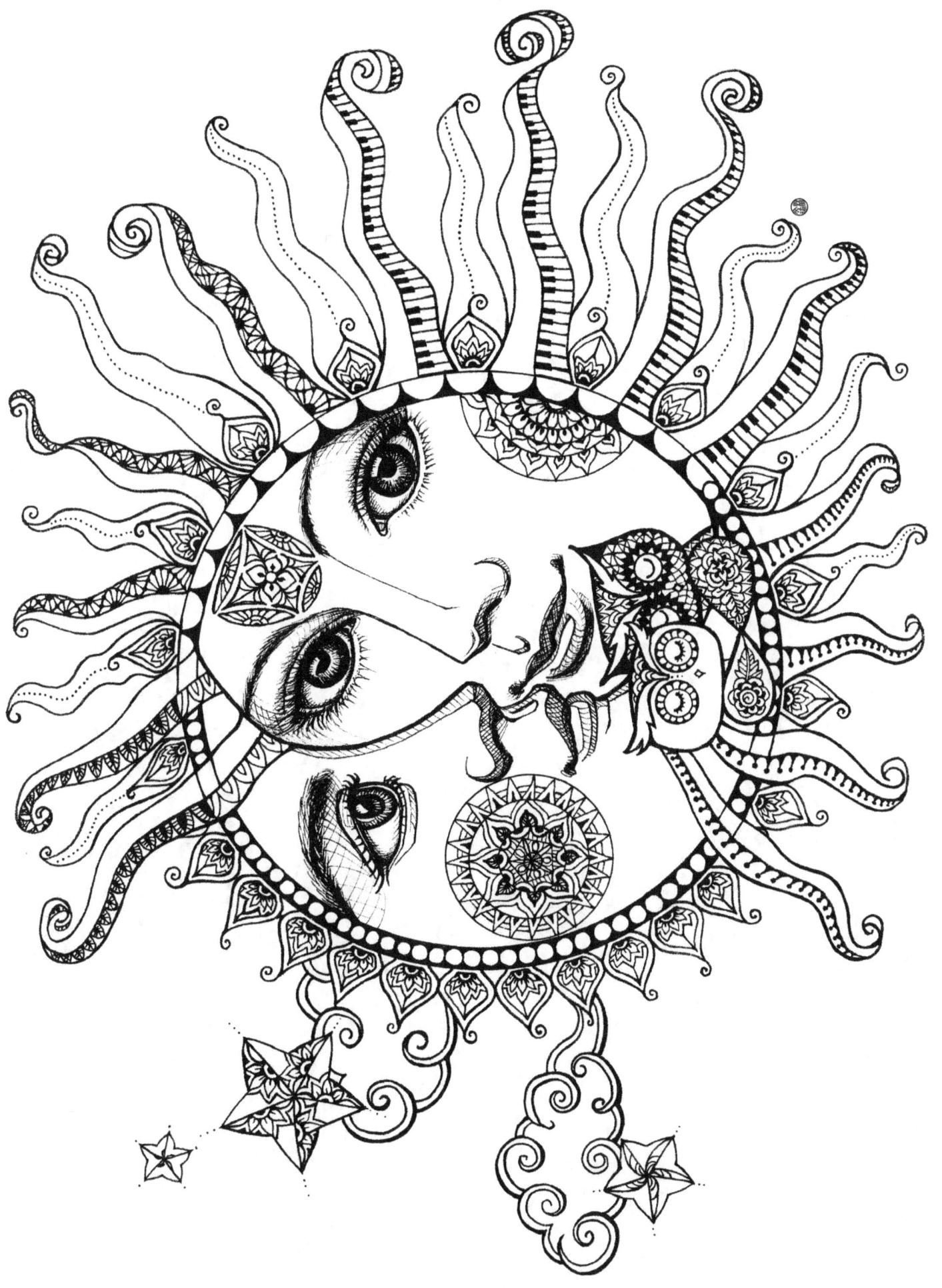

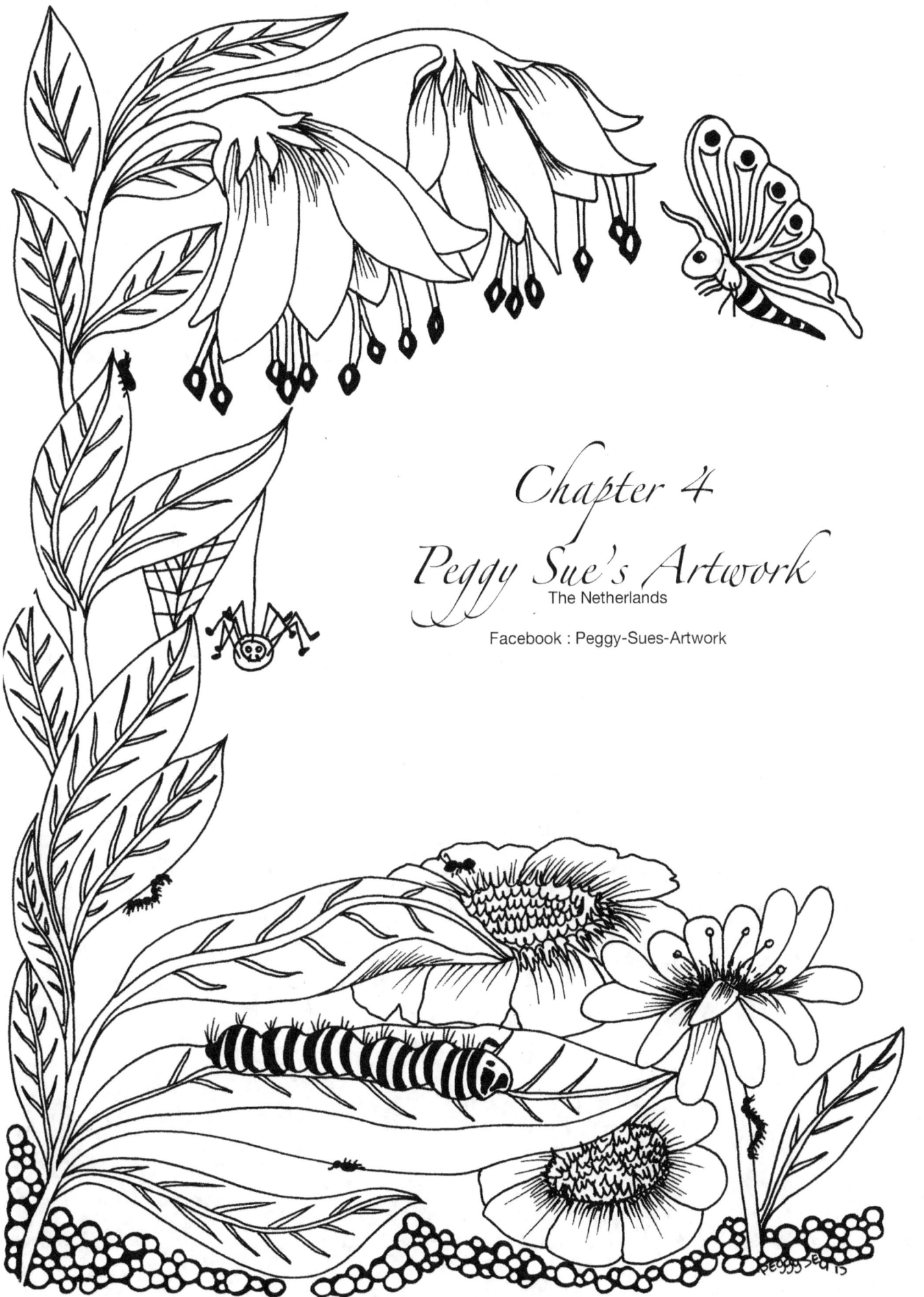

Chapter 4
Peggy Sue's Artwork
The Netherlands

Facebook : Peggy-Sues-Artwork

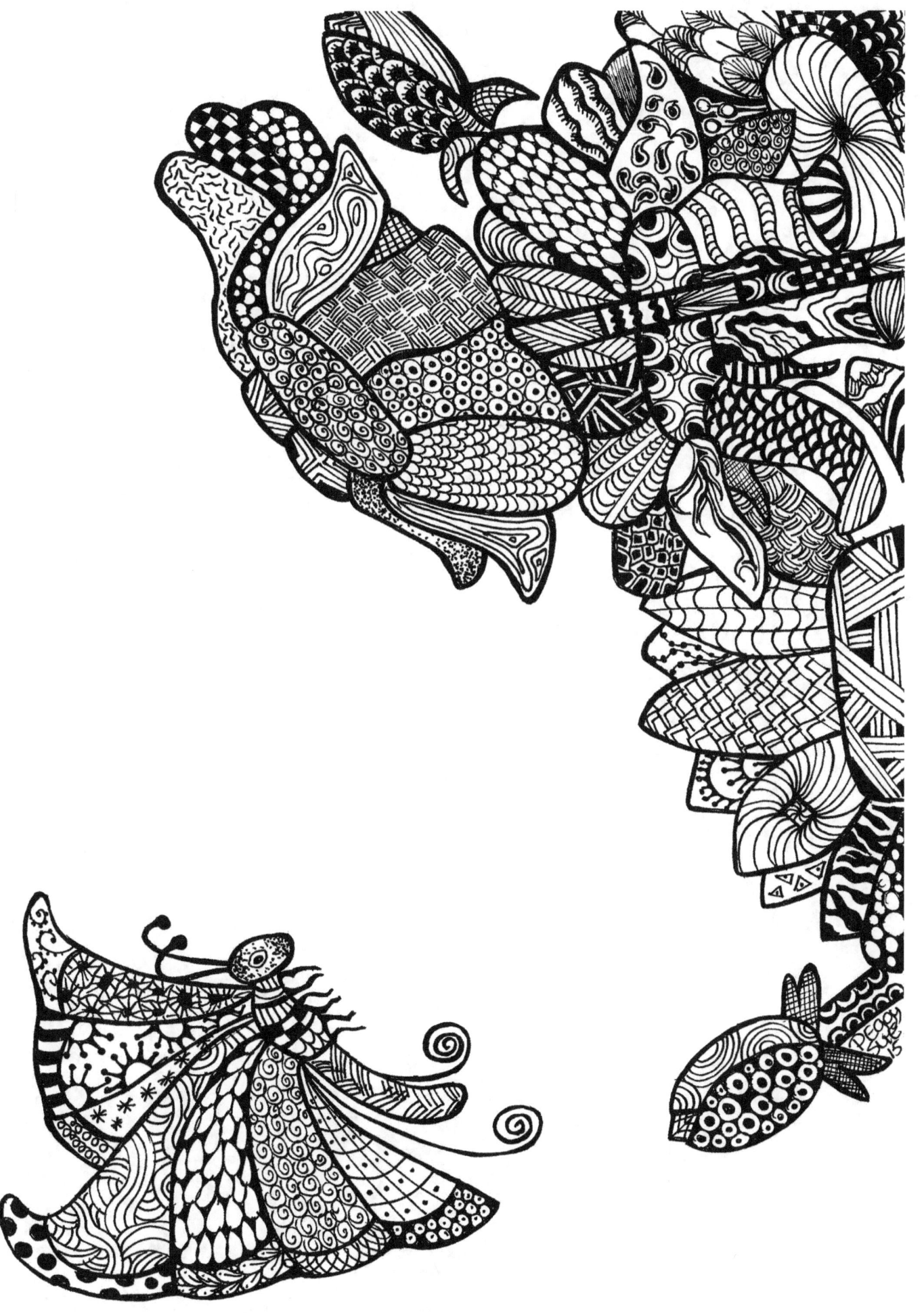

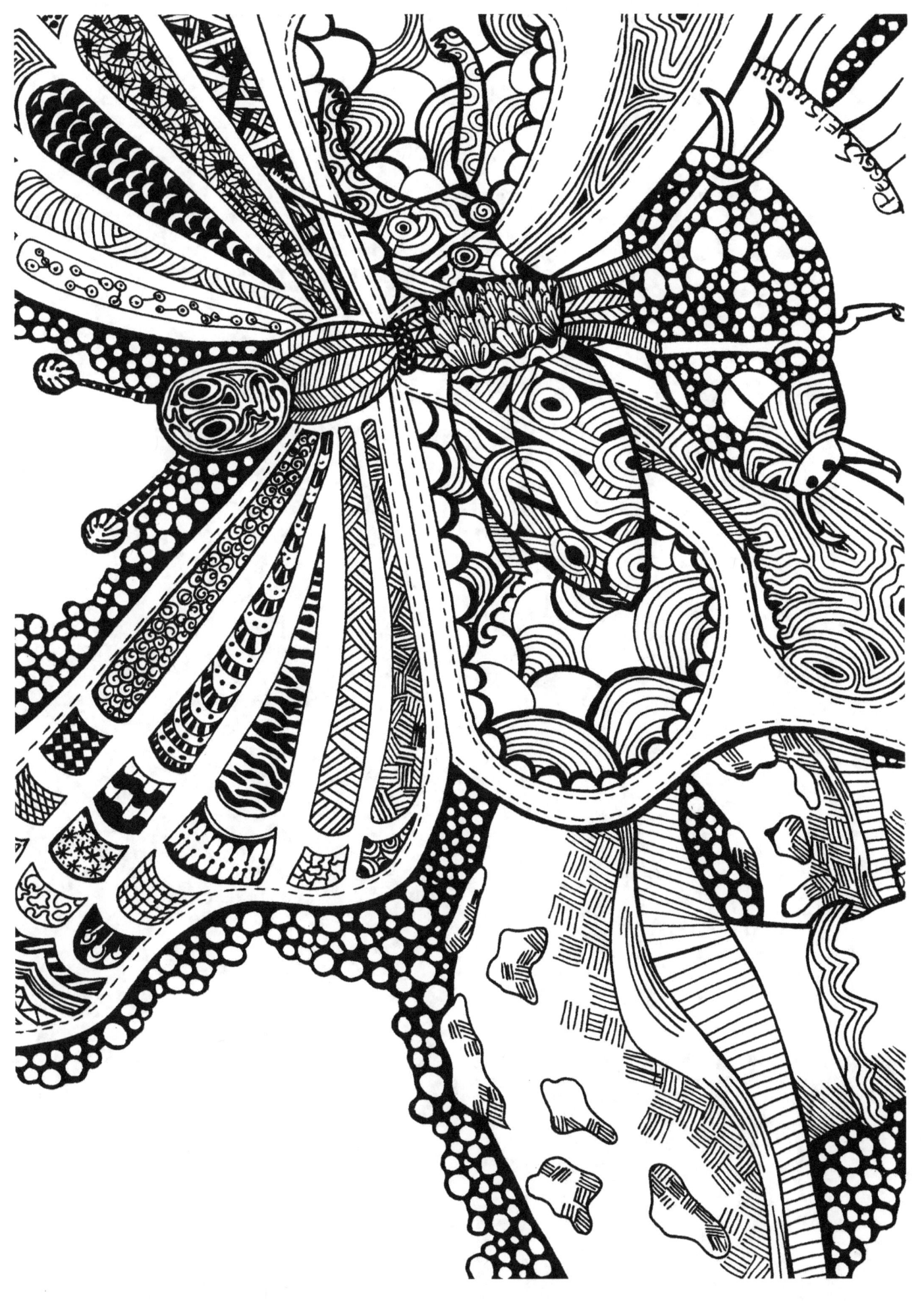

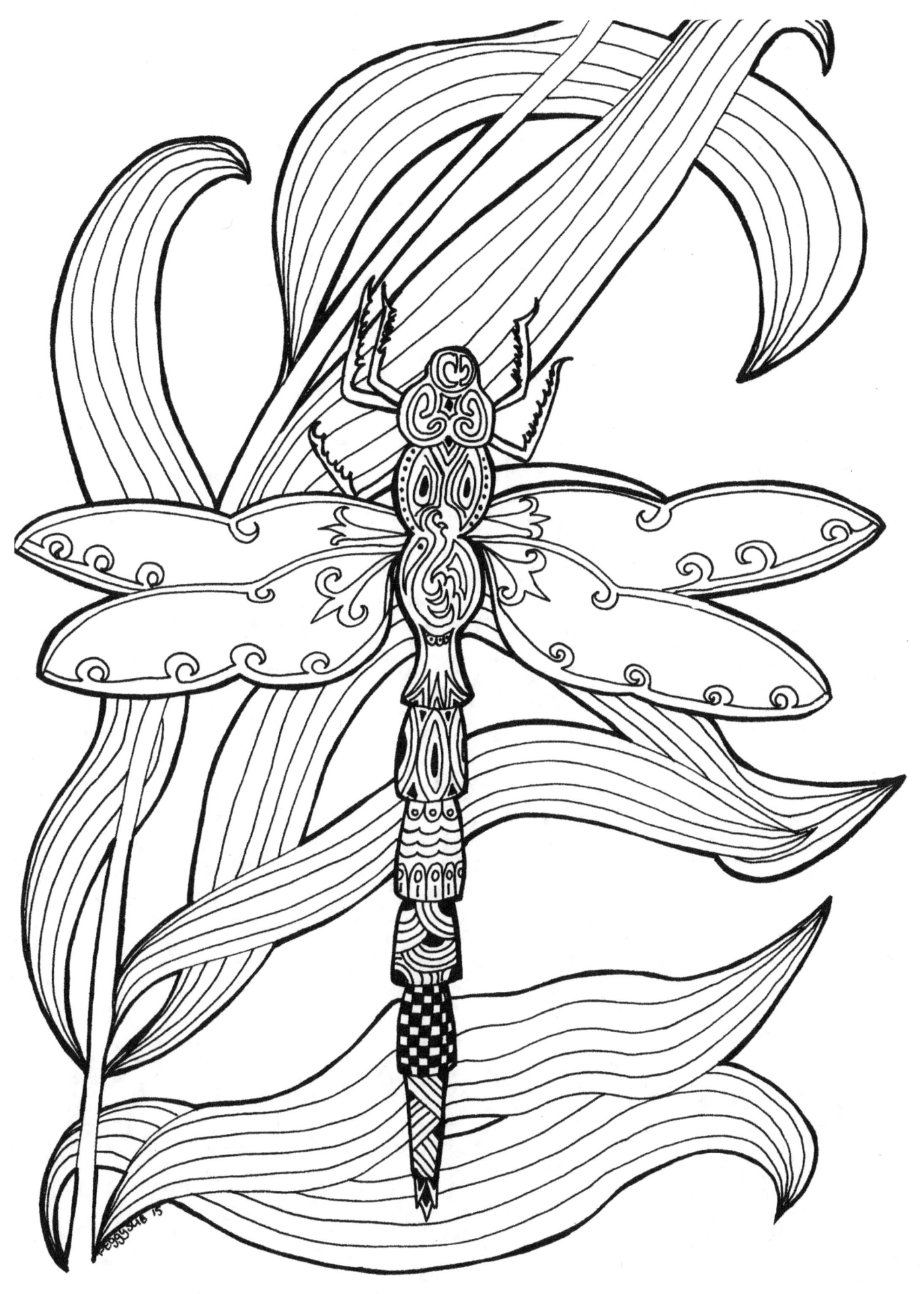

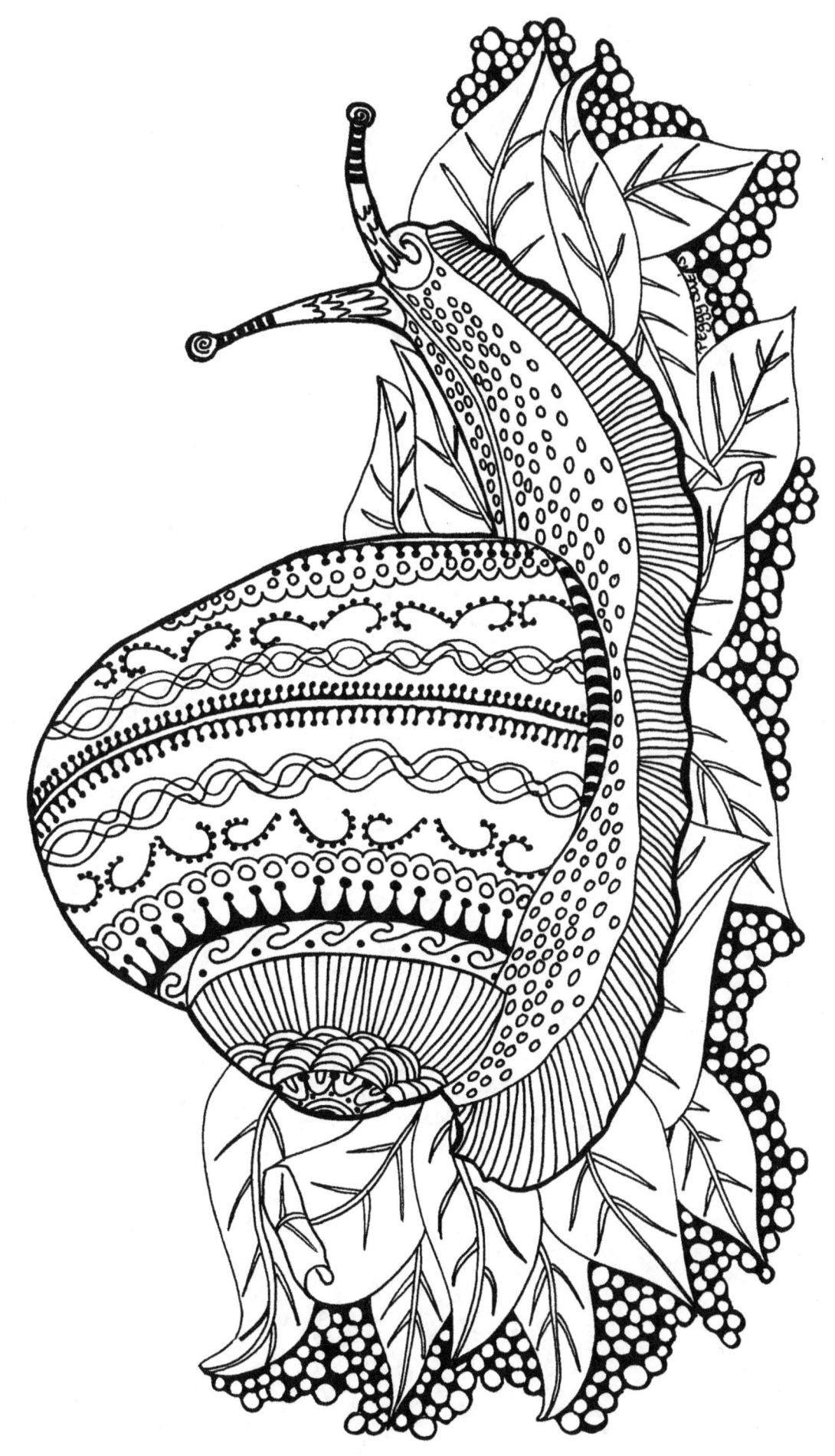

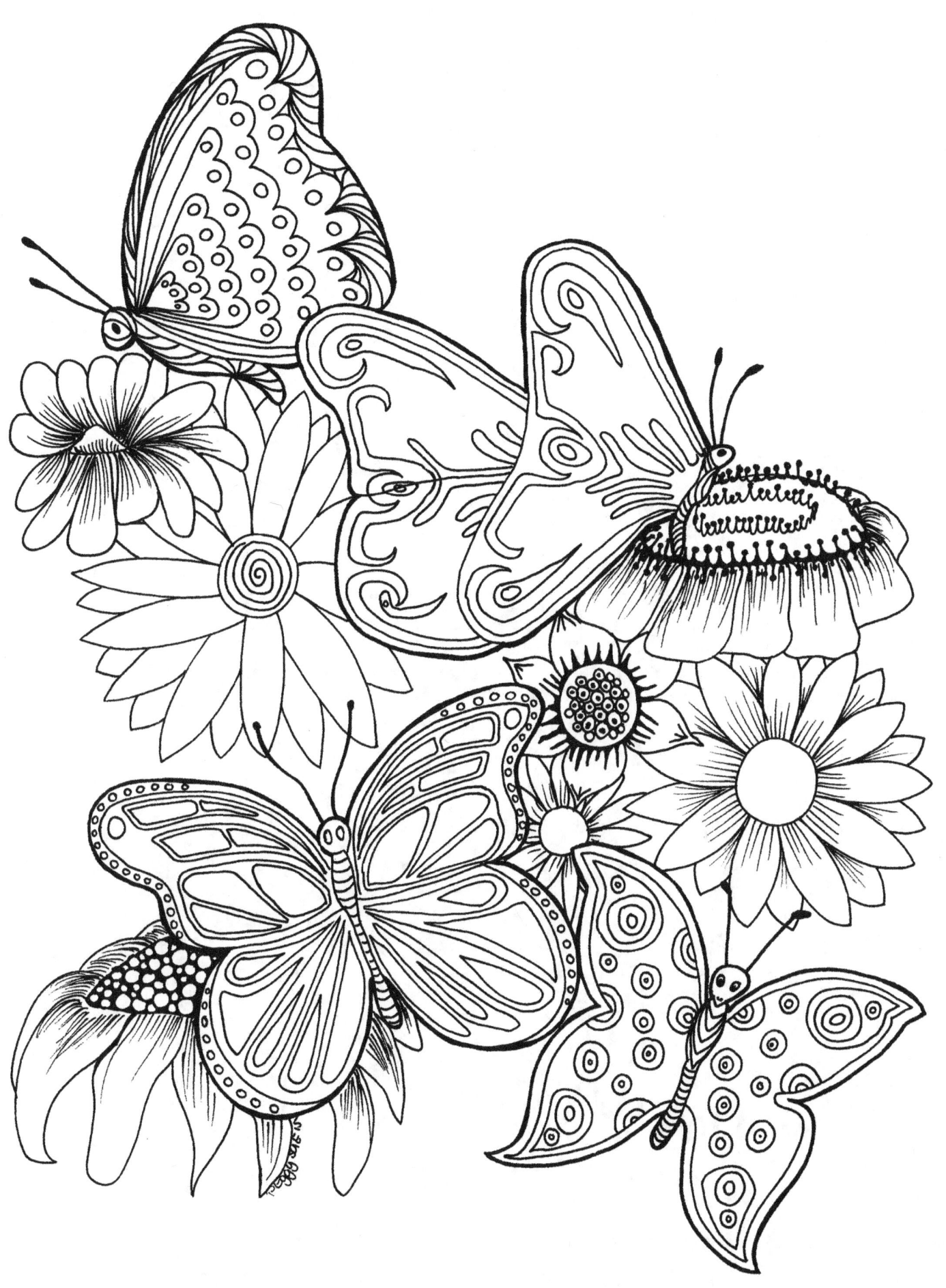

Chapter 5
Yaya
France

Facebook : Les-gribouillis-de-yaya-georgia-merino

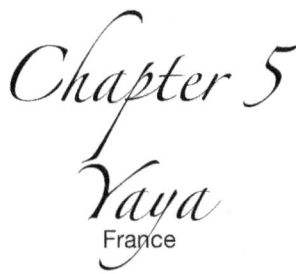

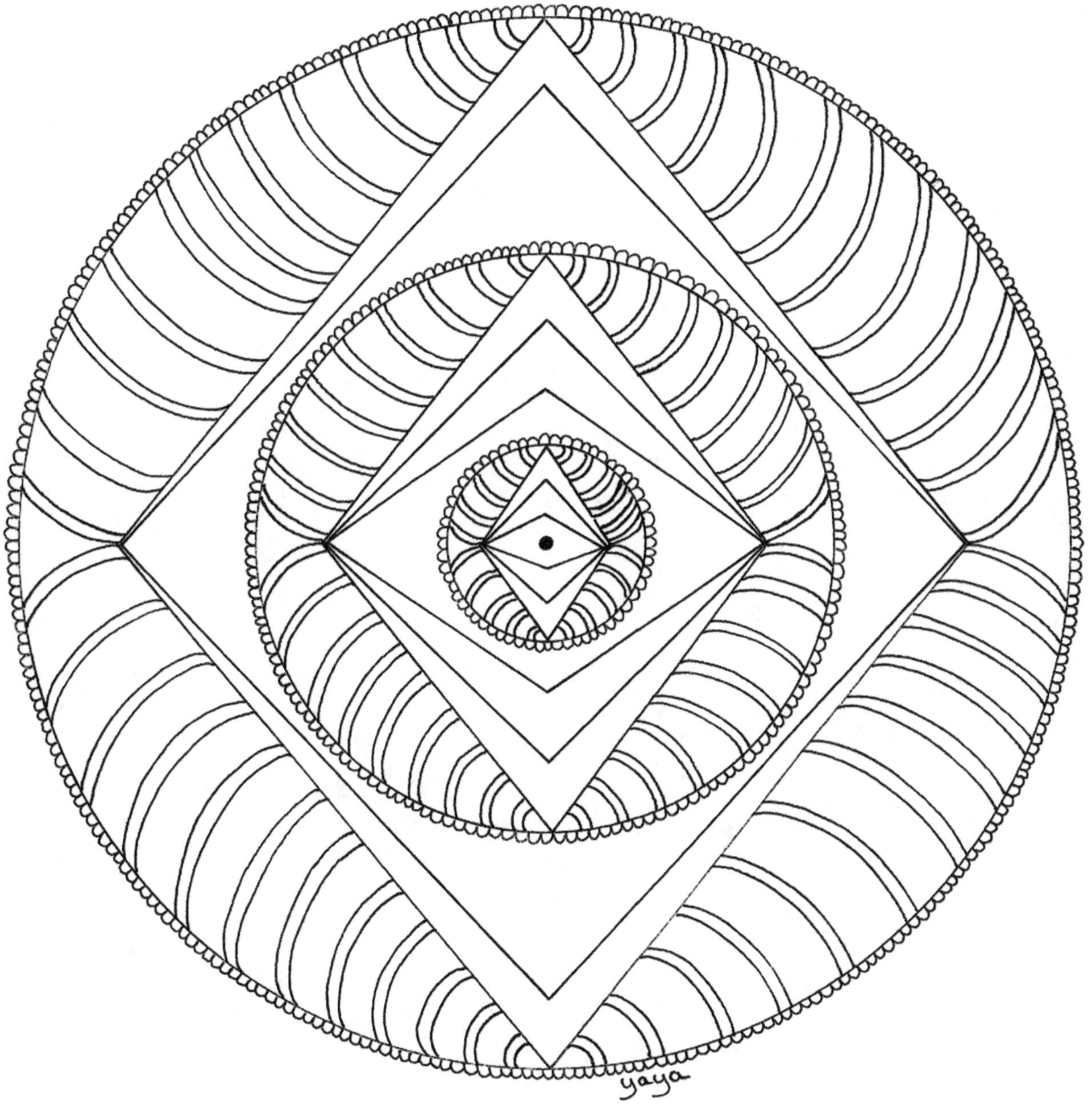

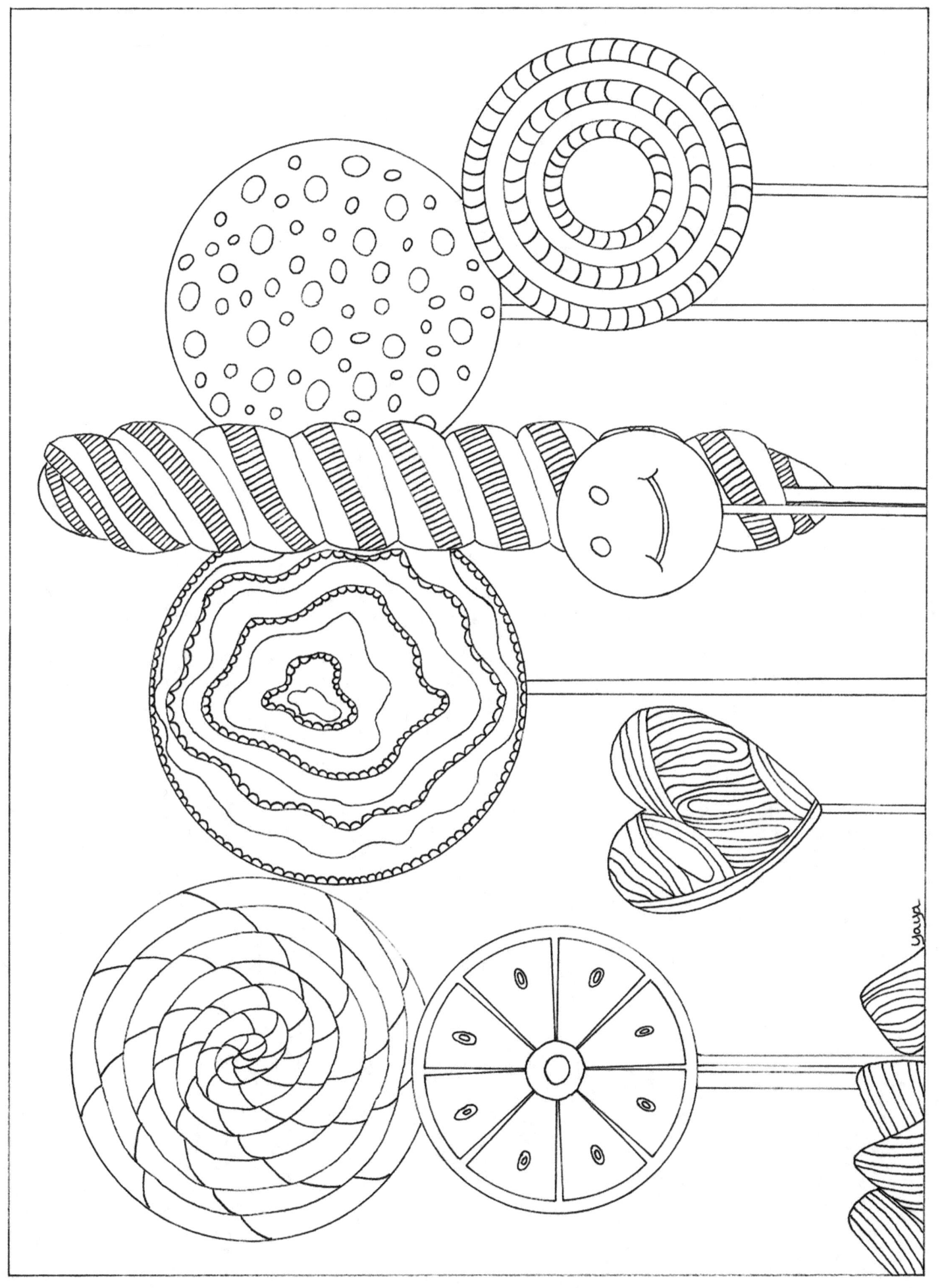

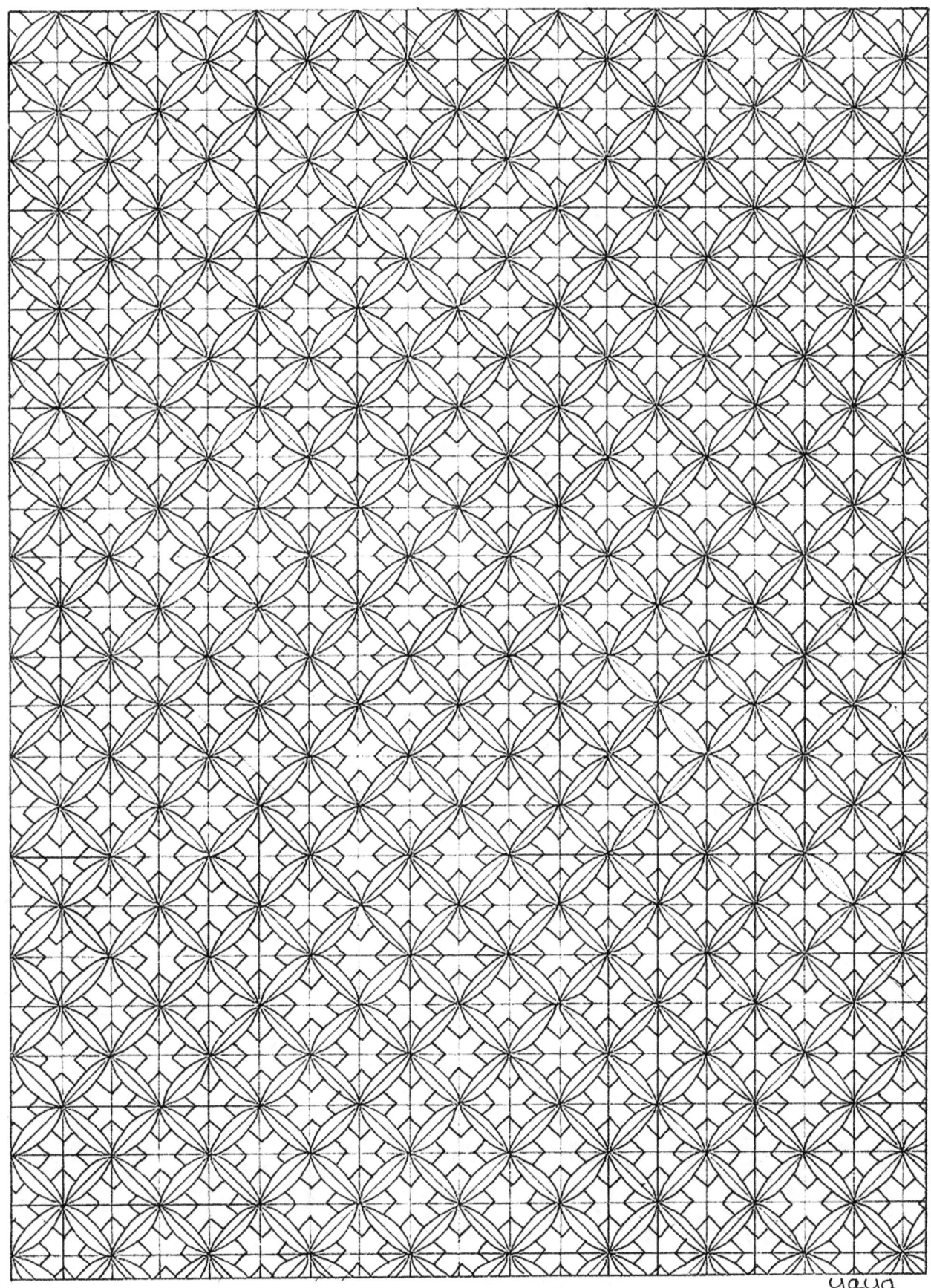

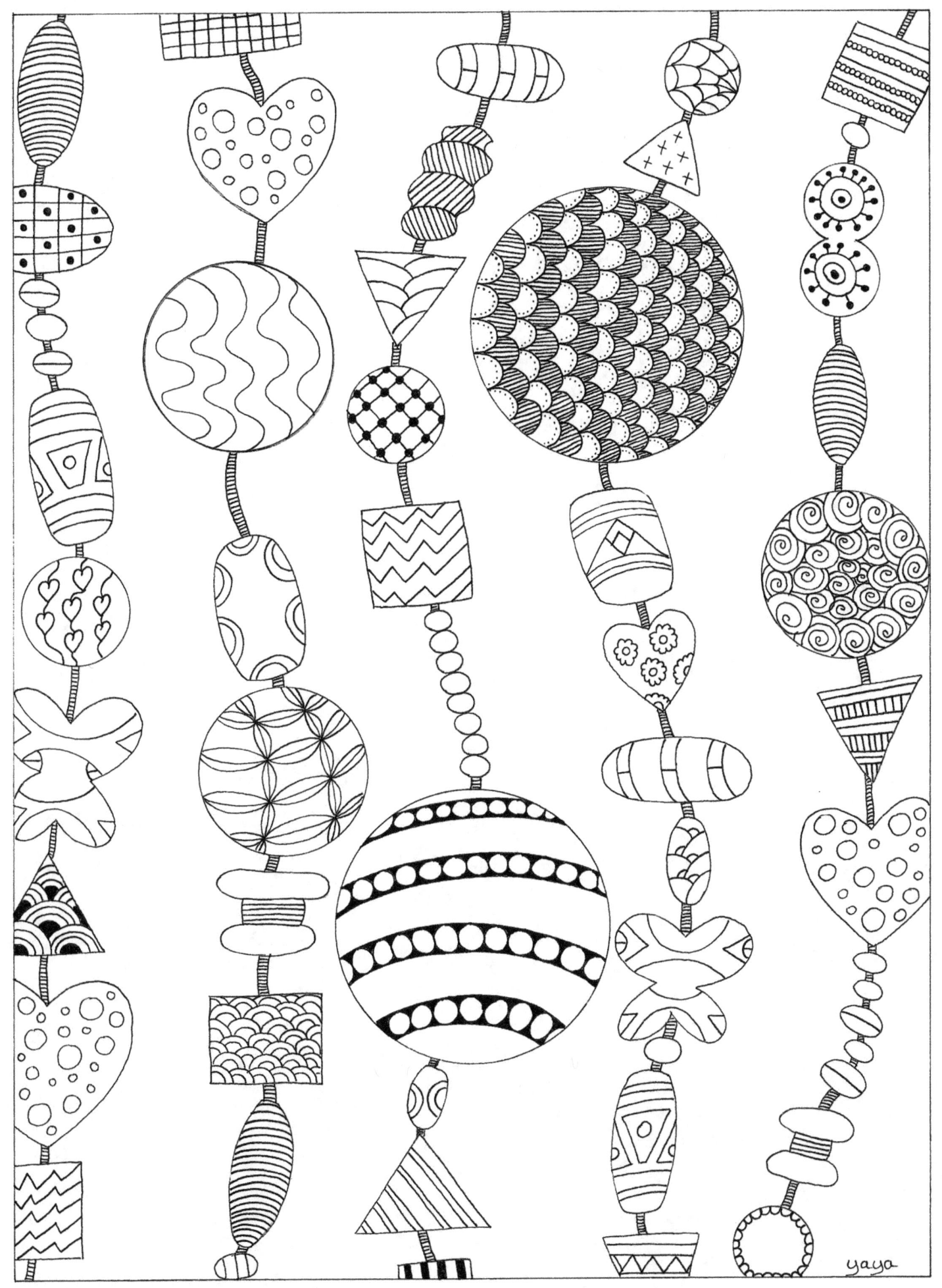

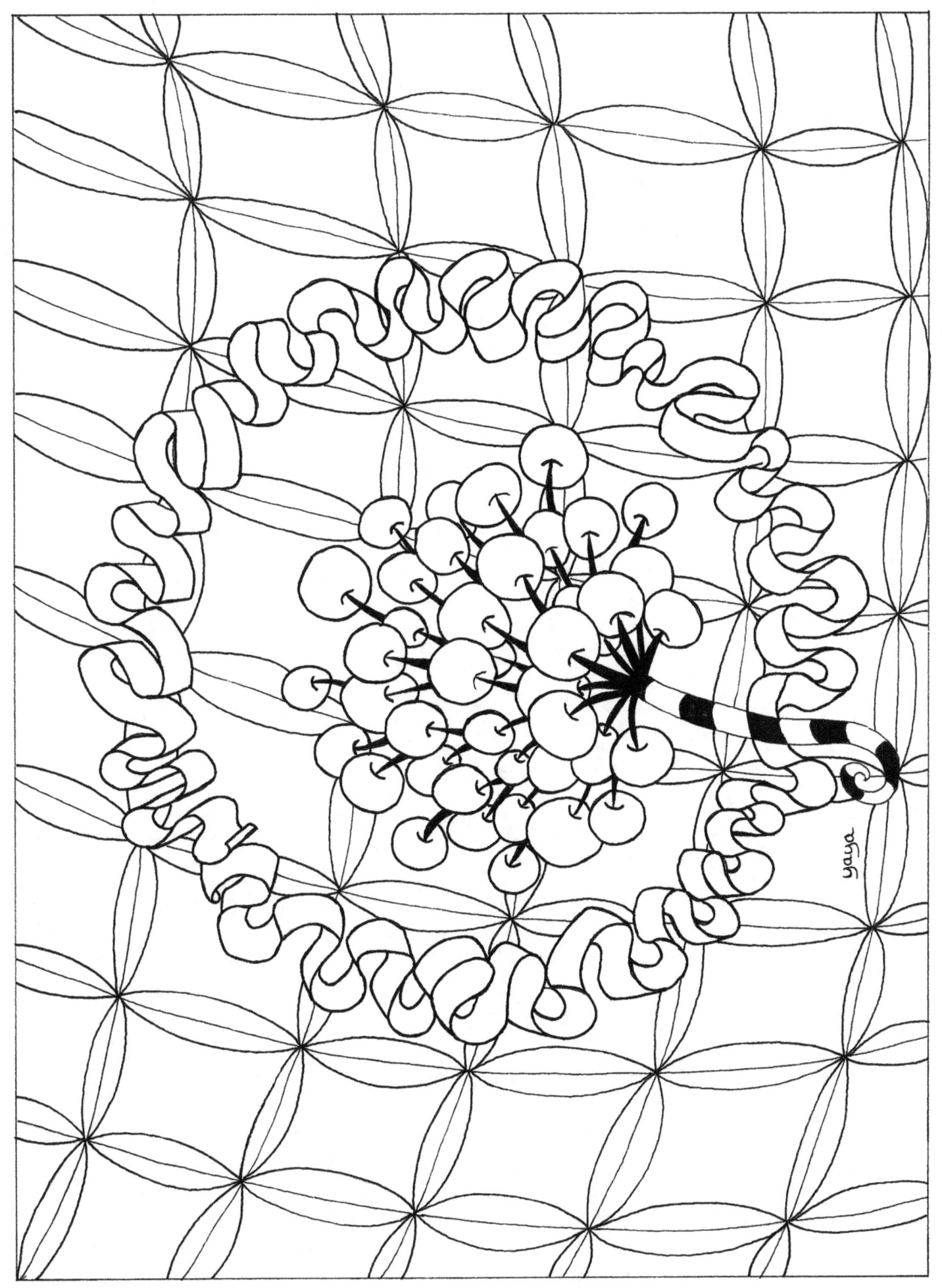

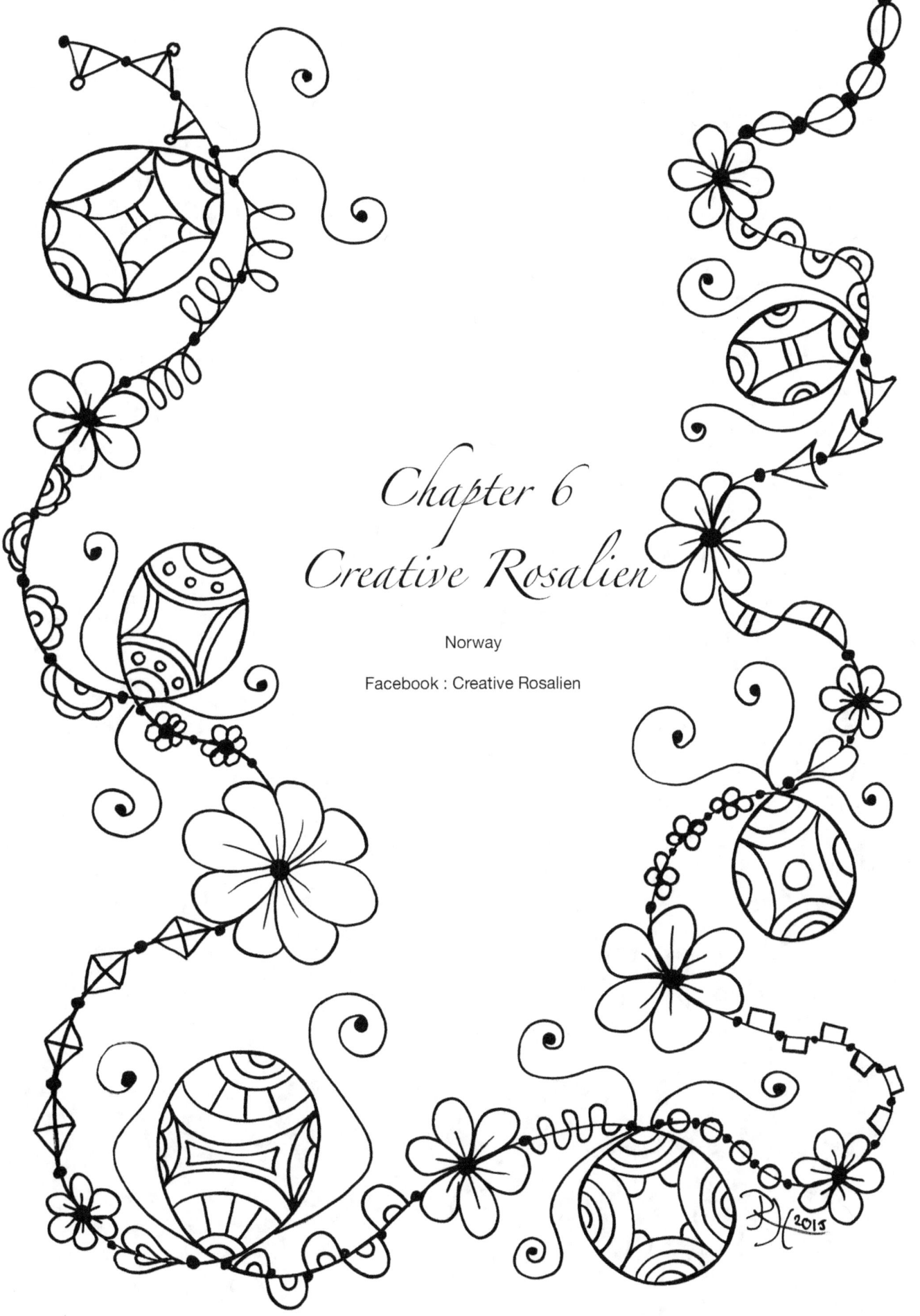

Chapter 6
Creative Rosalien

Norway

Facebook : Creative Rosalien

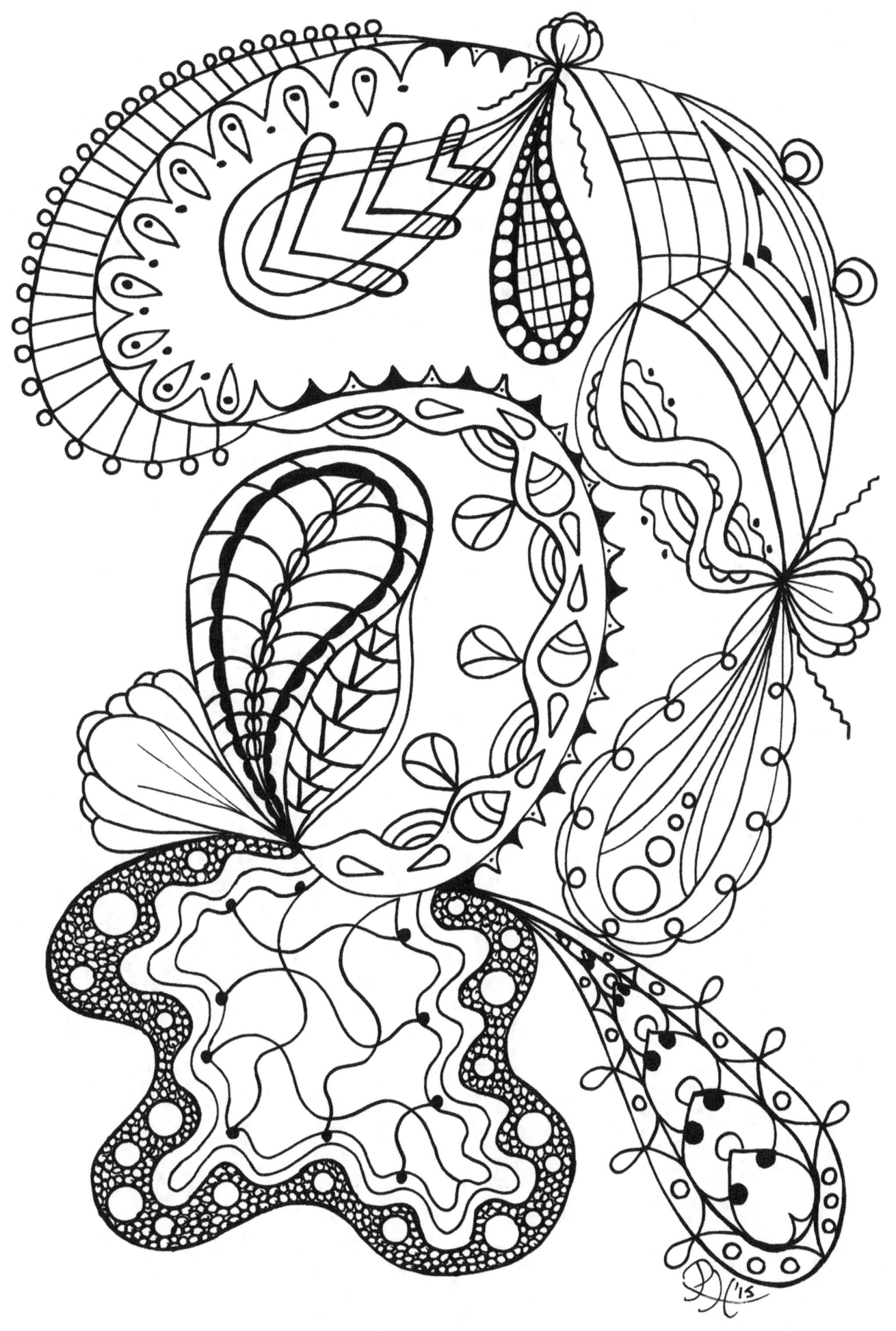

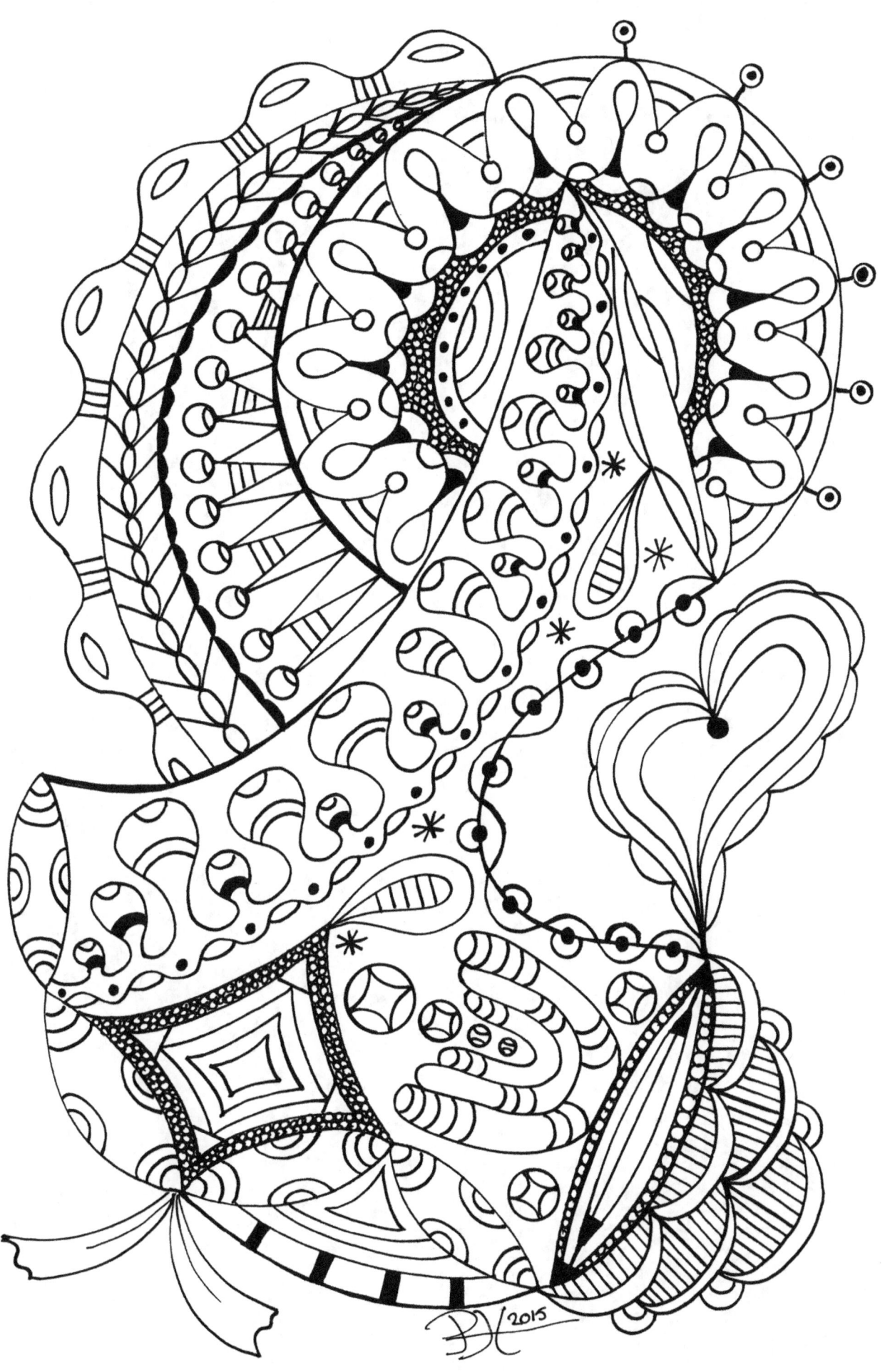

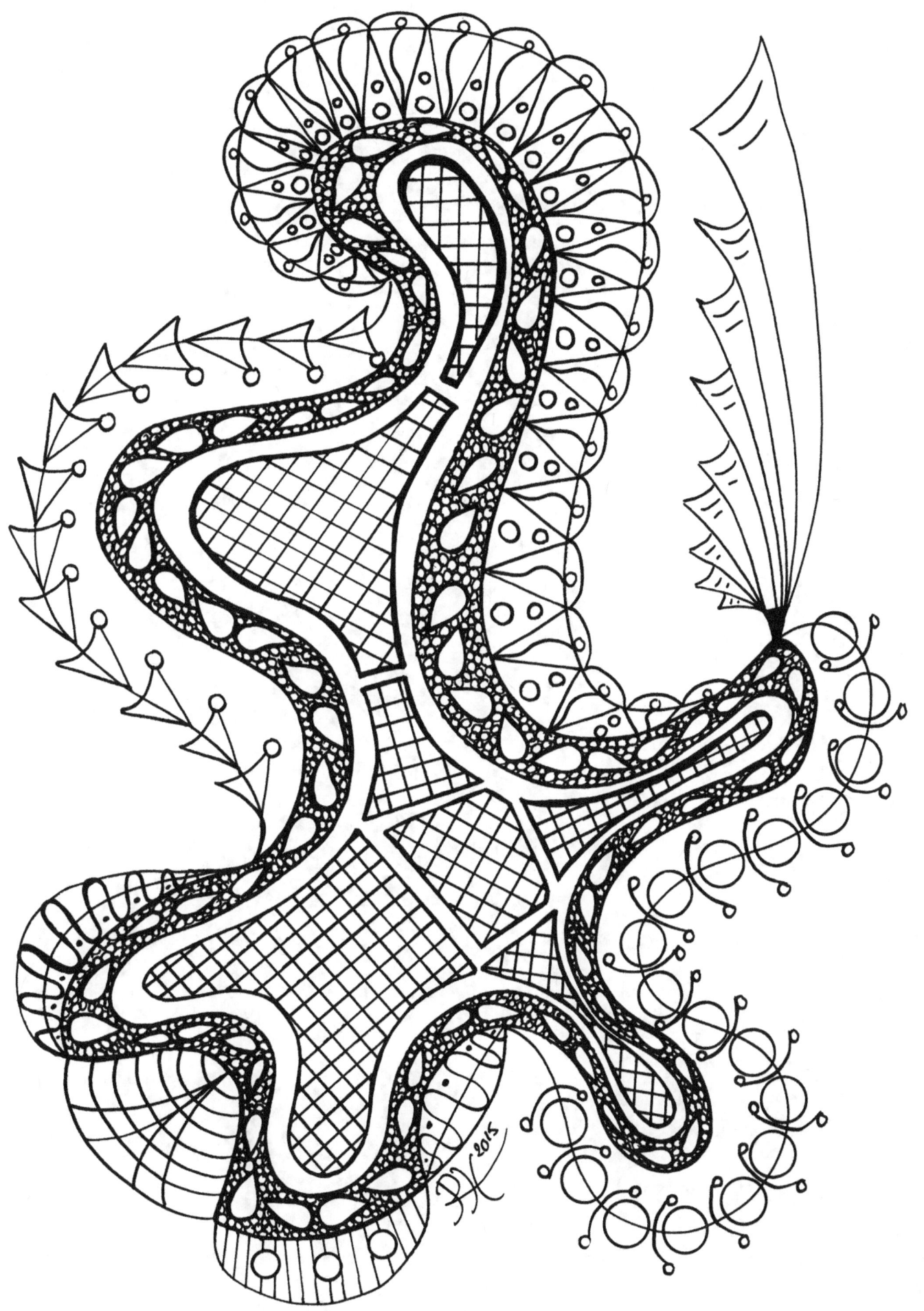

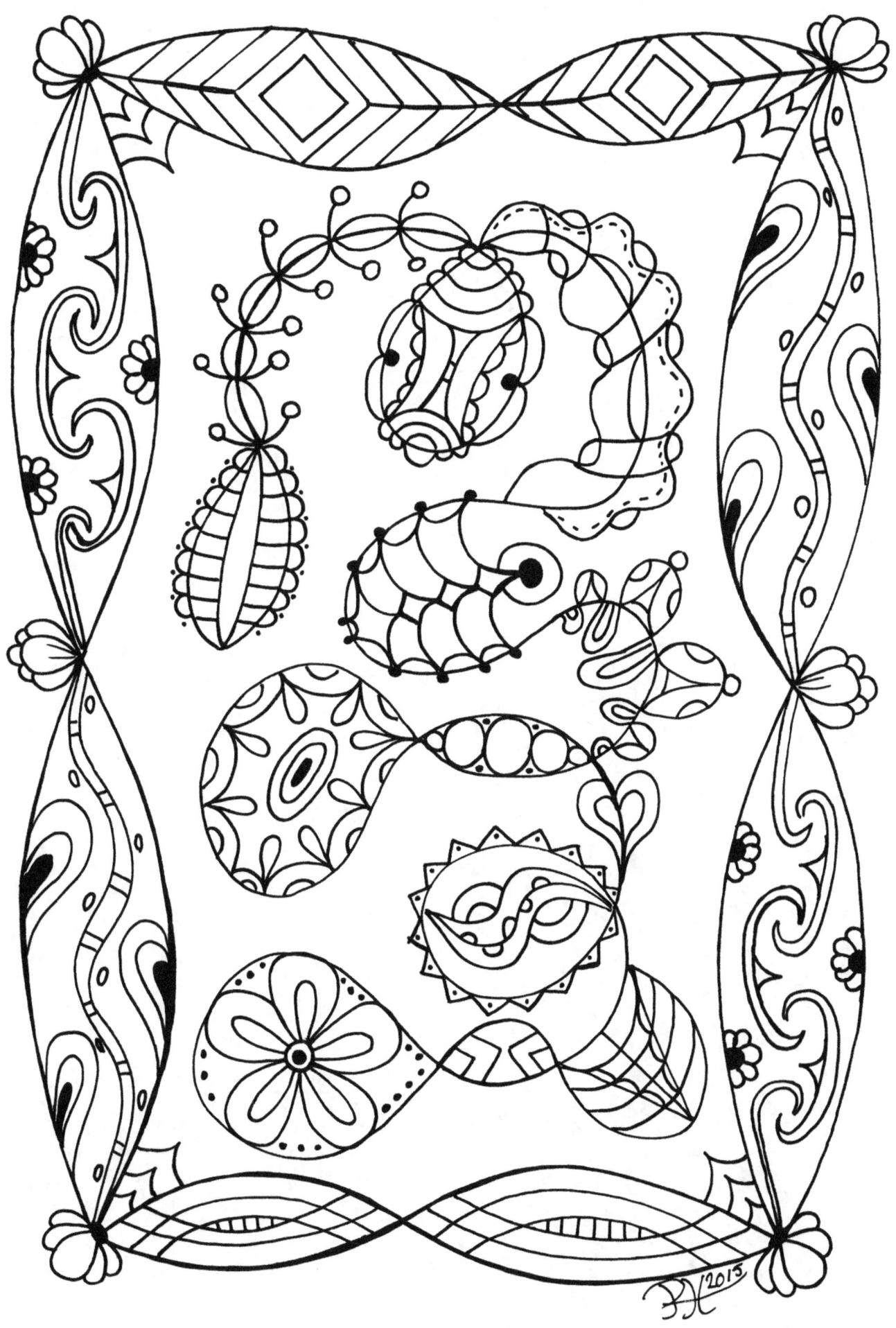

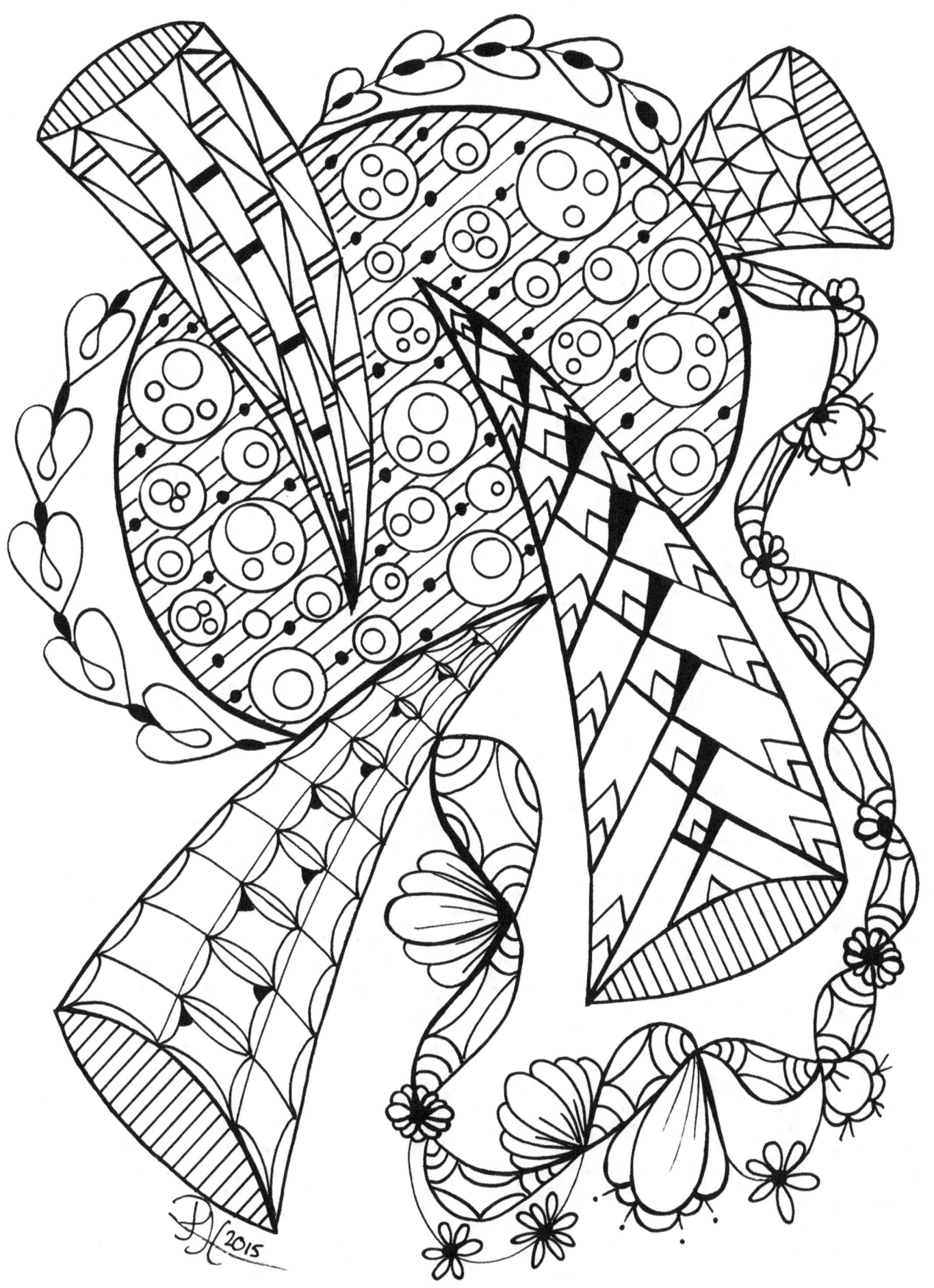

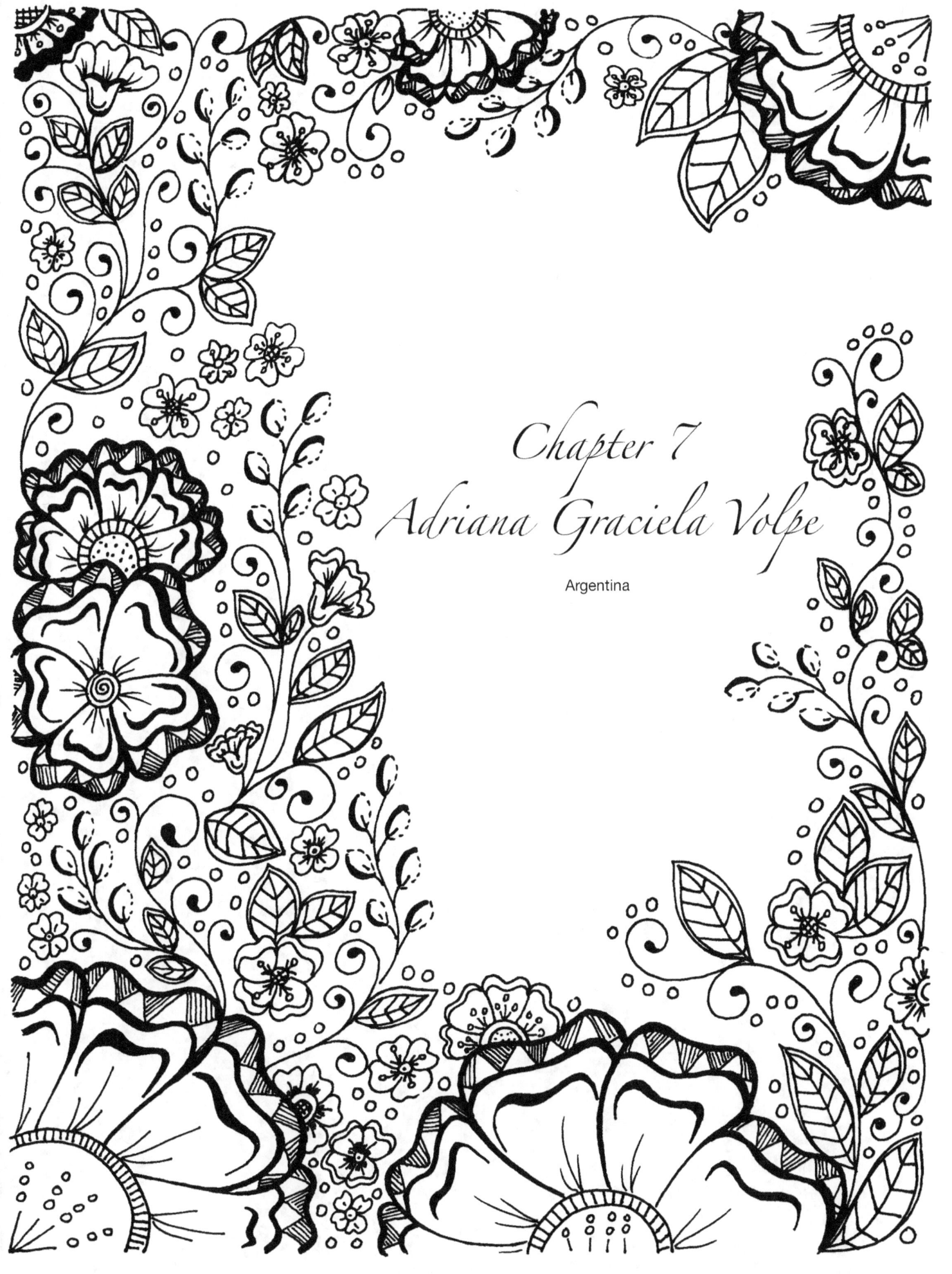

Chapter 7
Adriana Graciela Volpe
Argentina

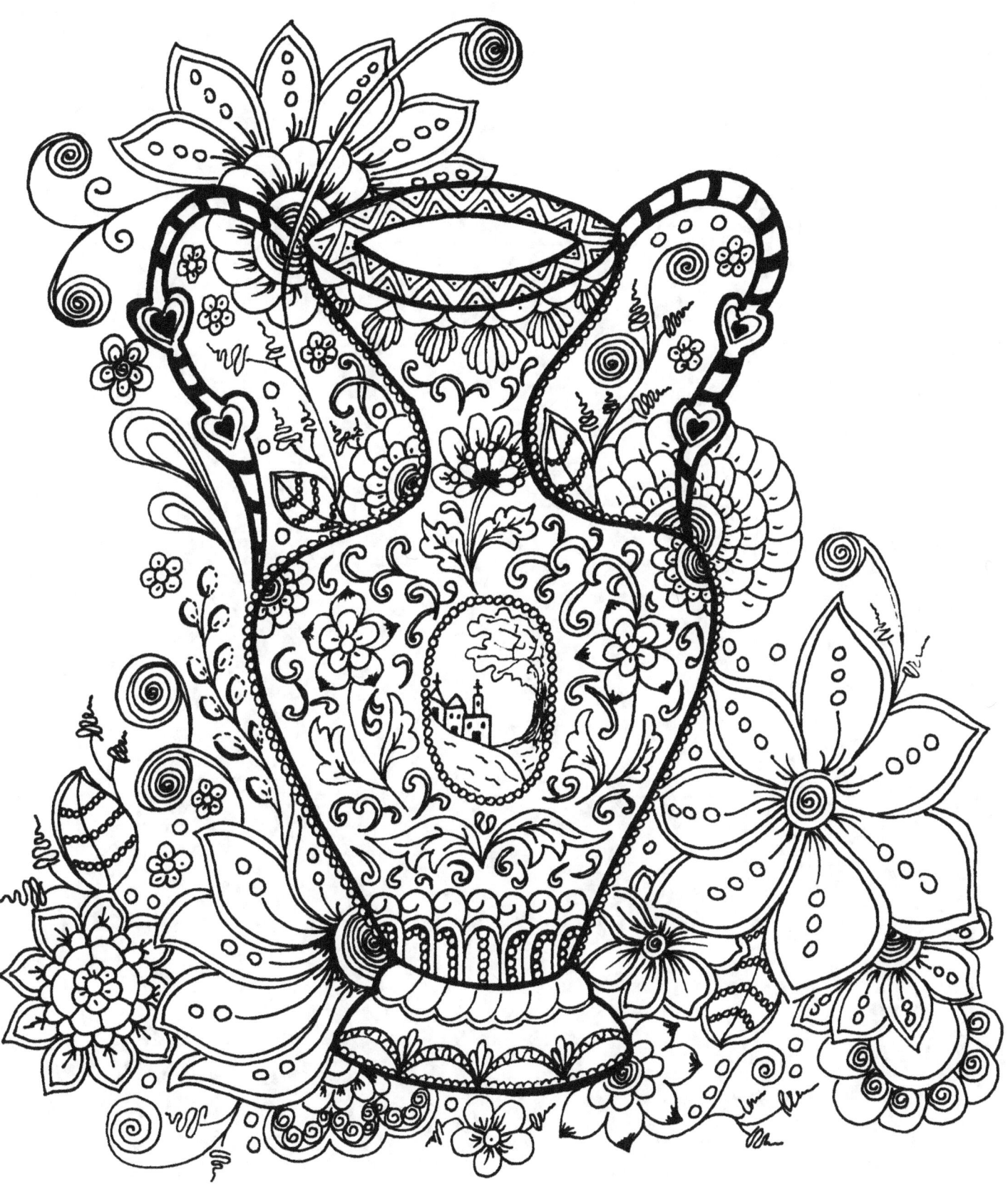

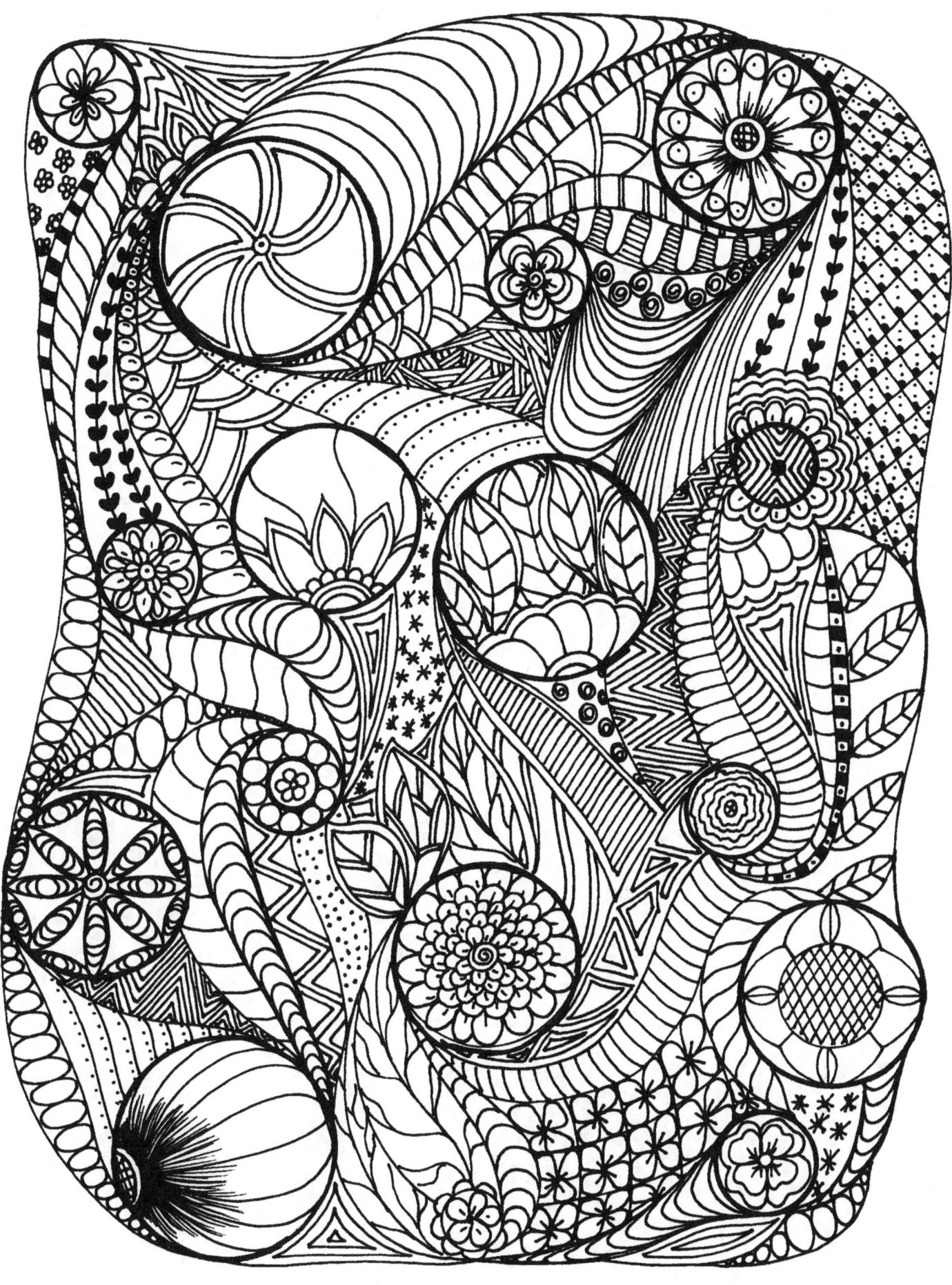

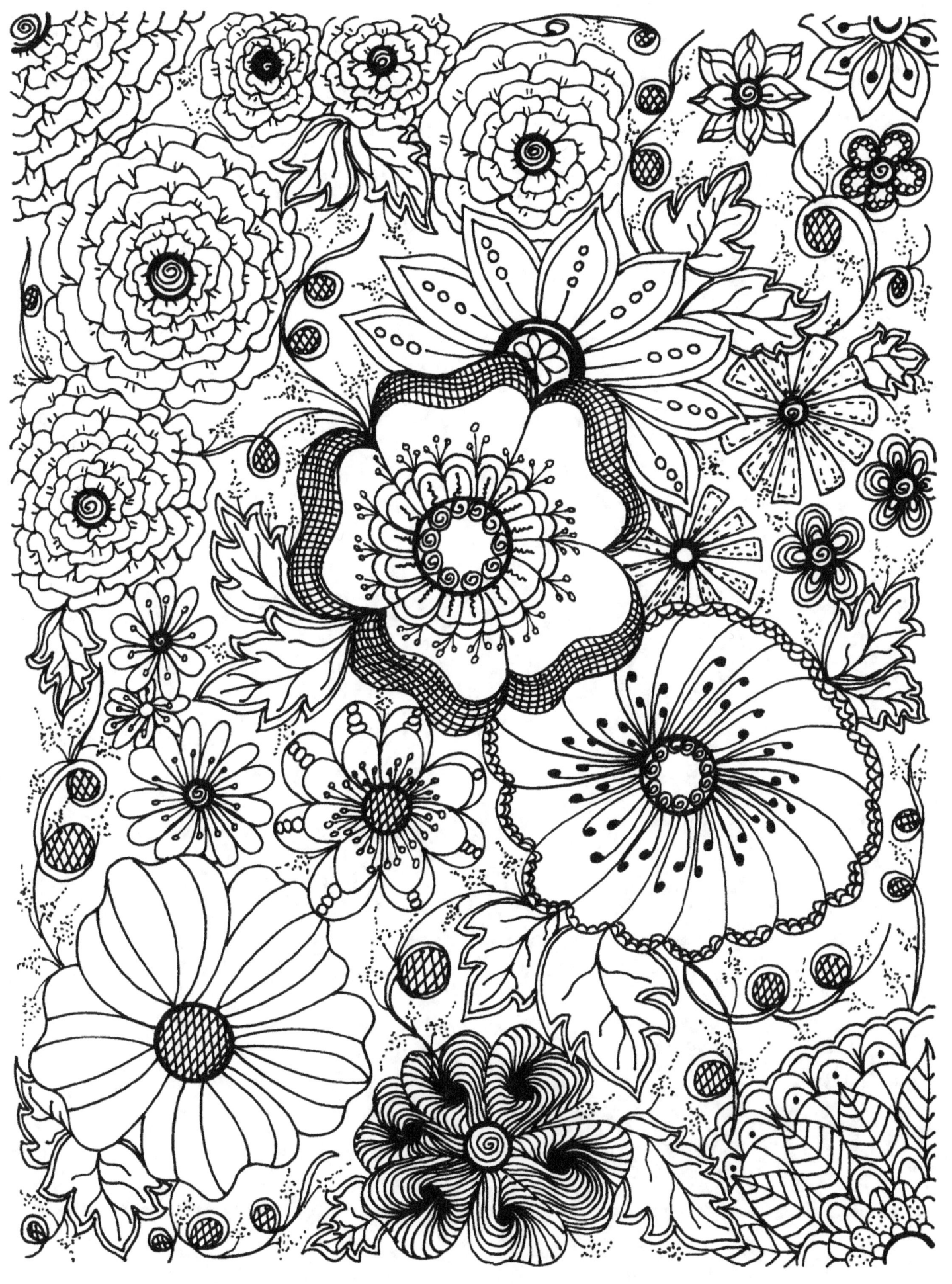

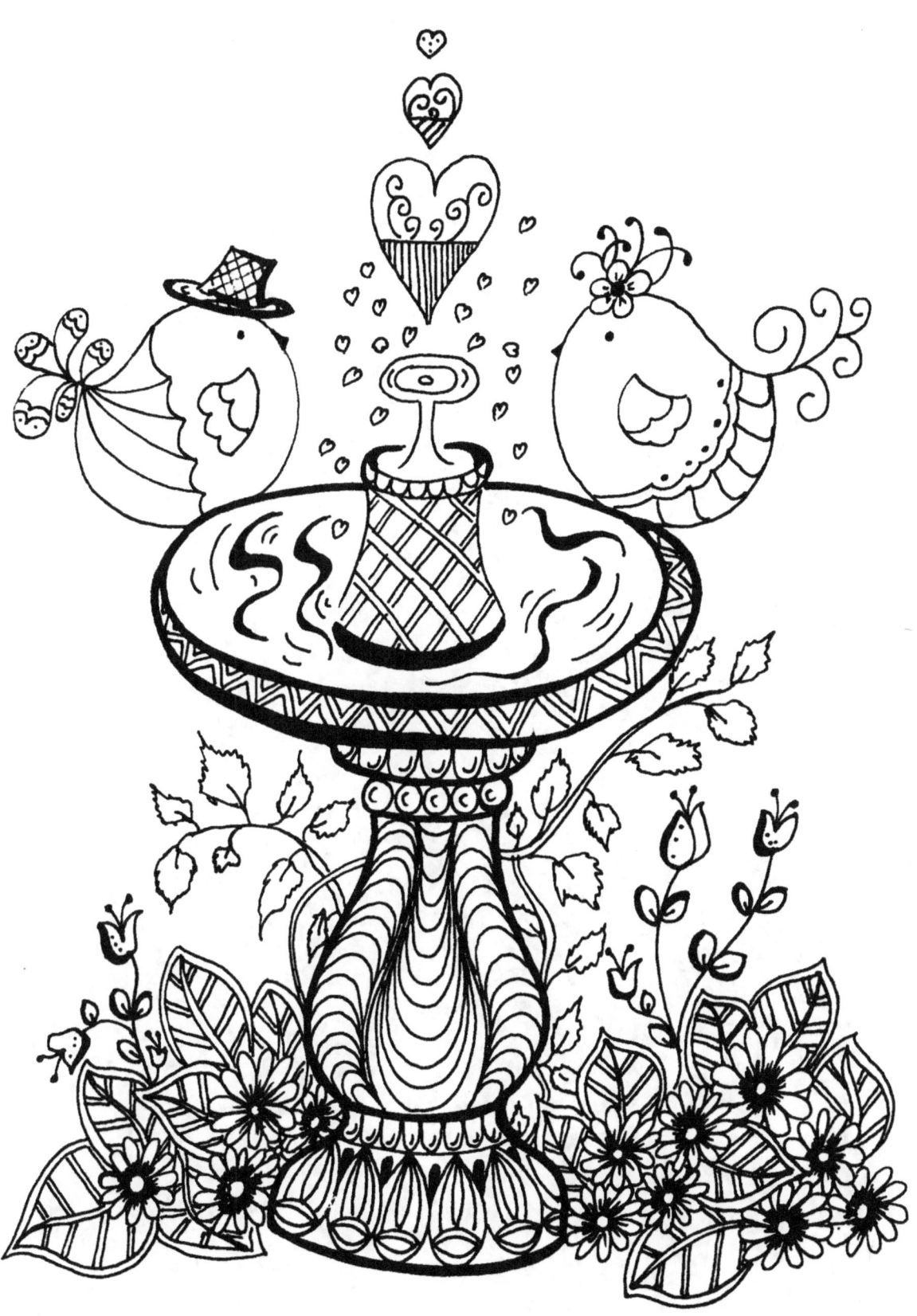

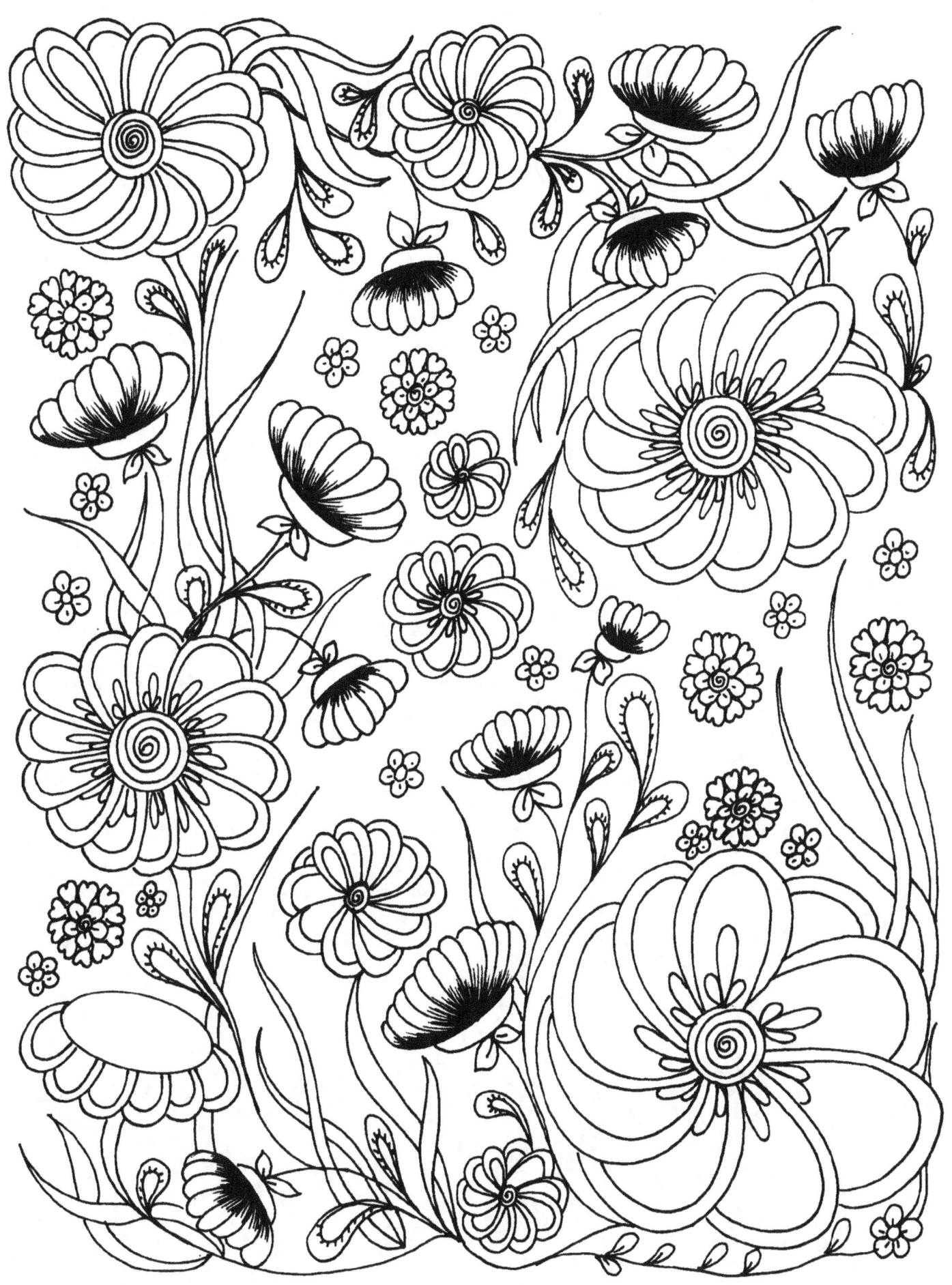

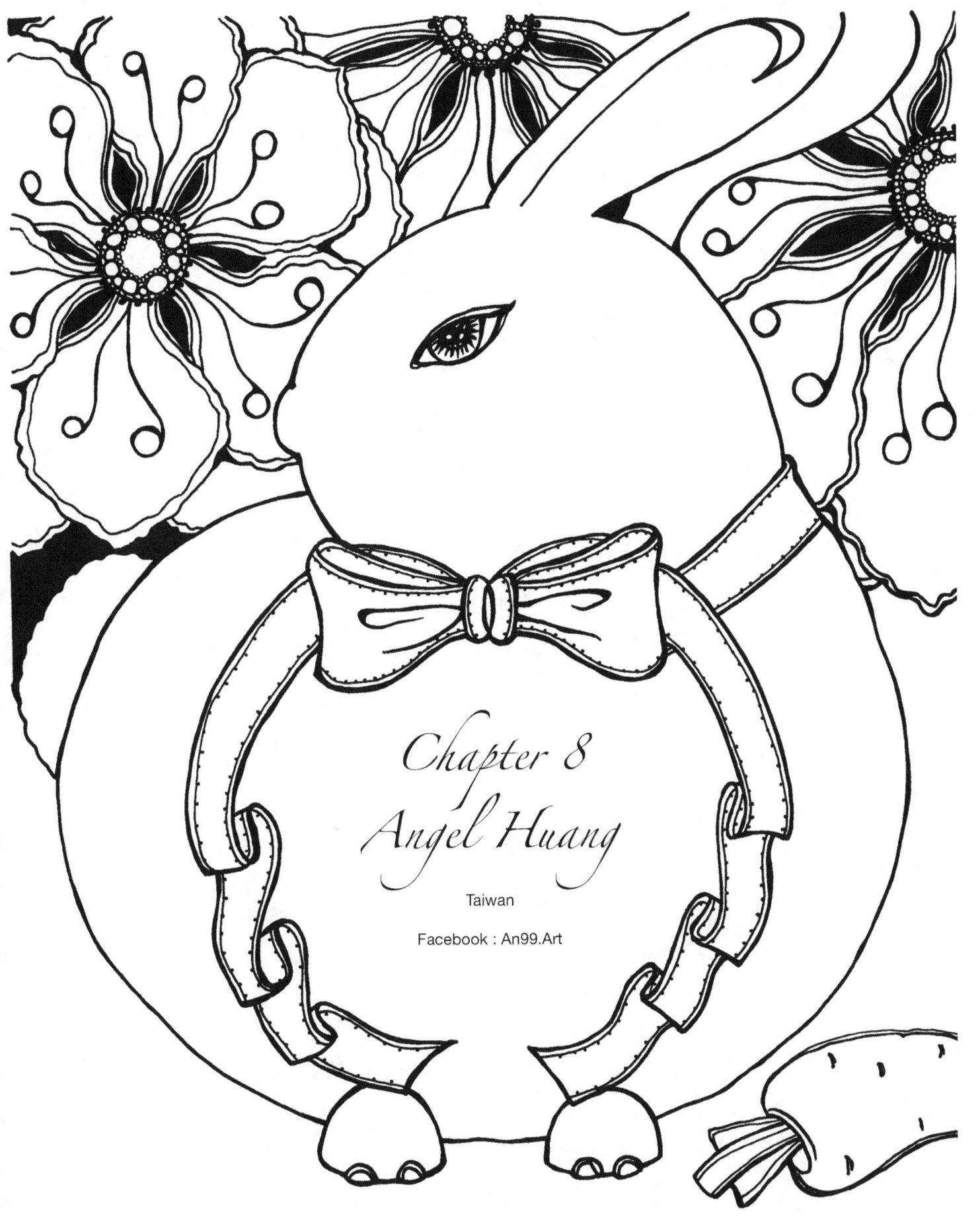

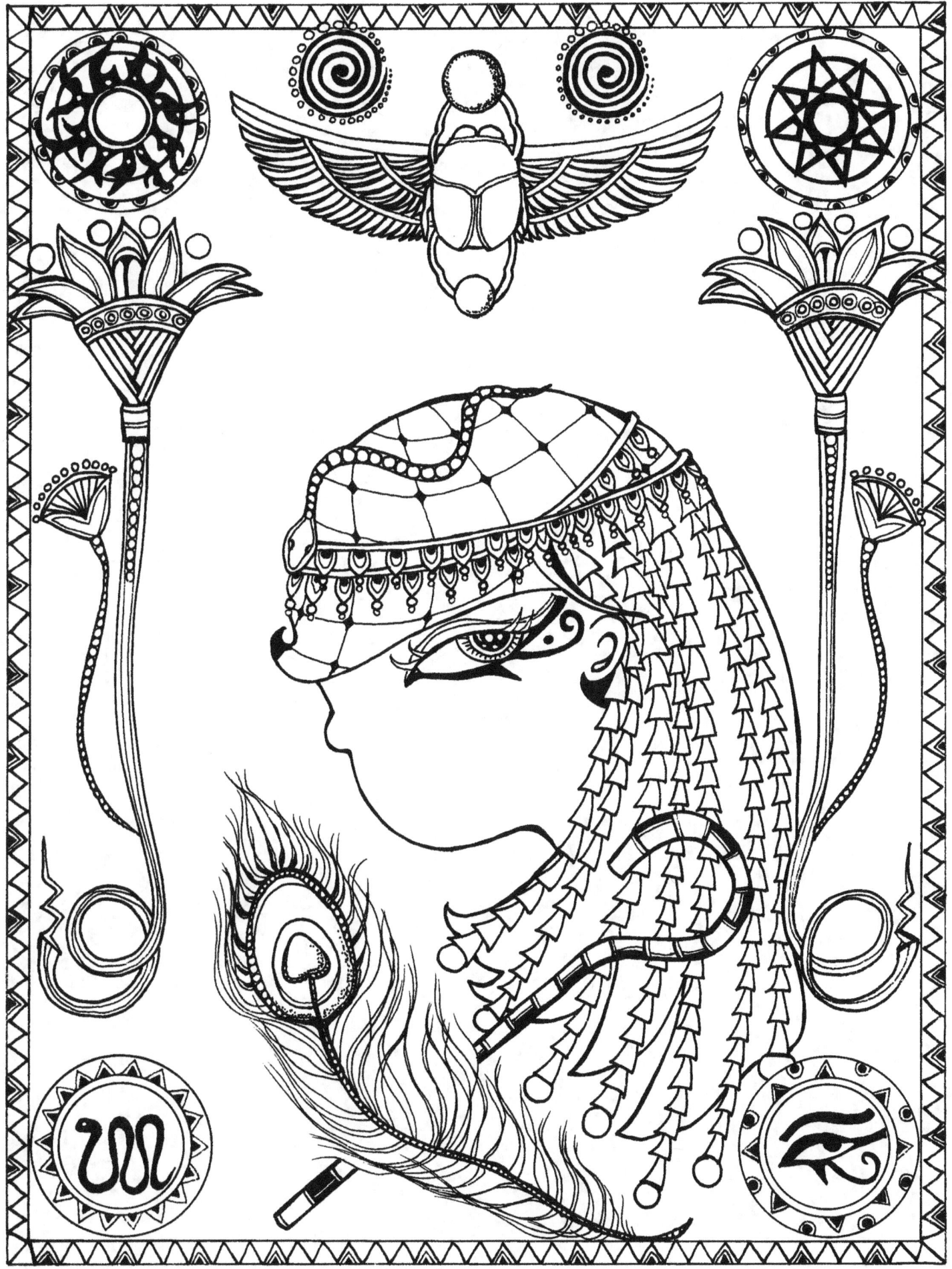

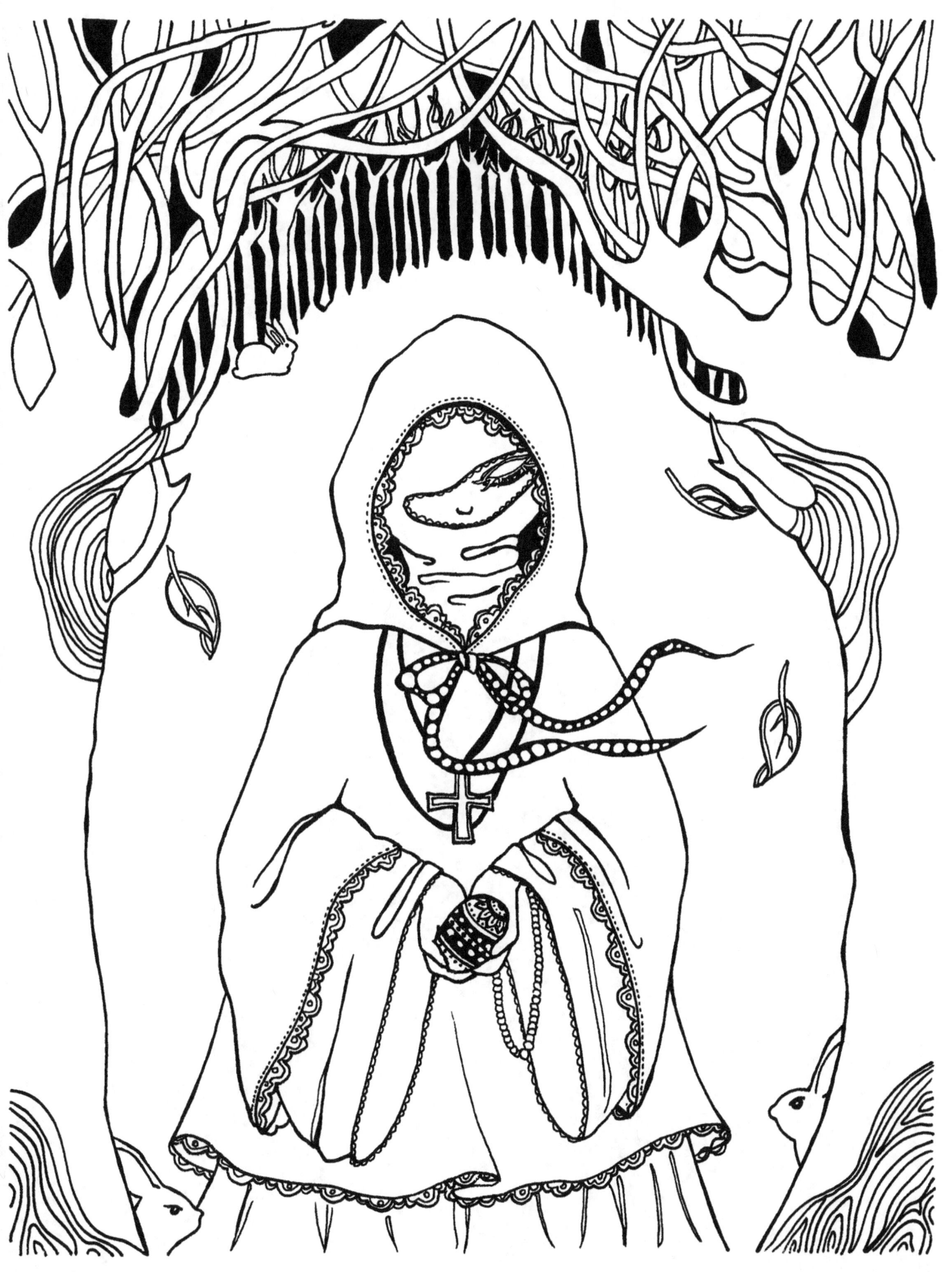

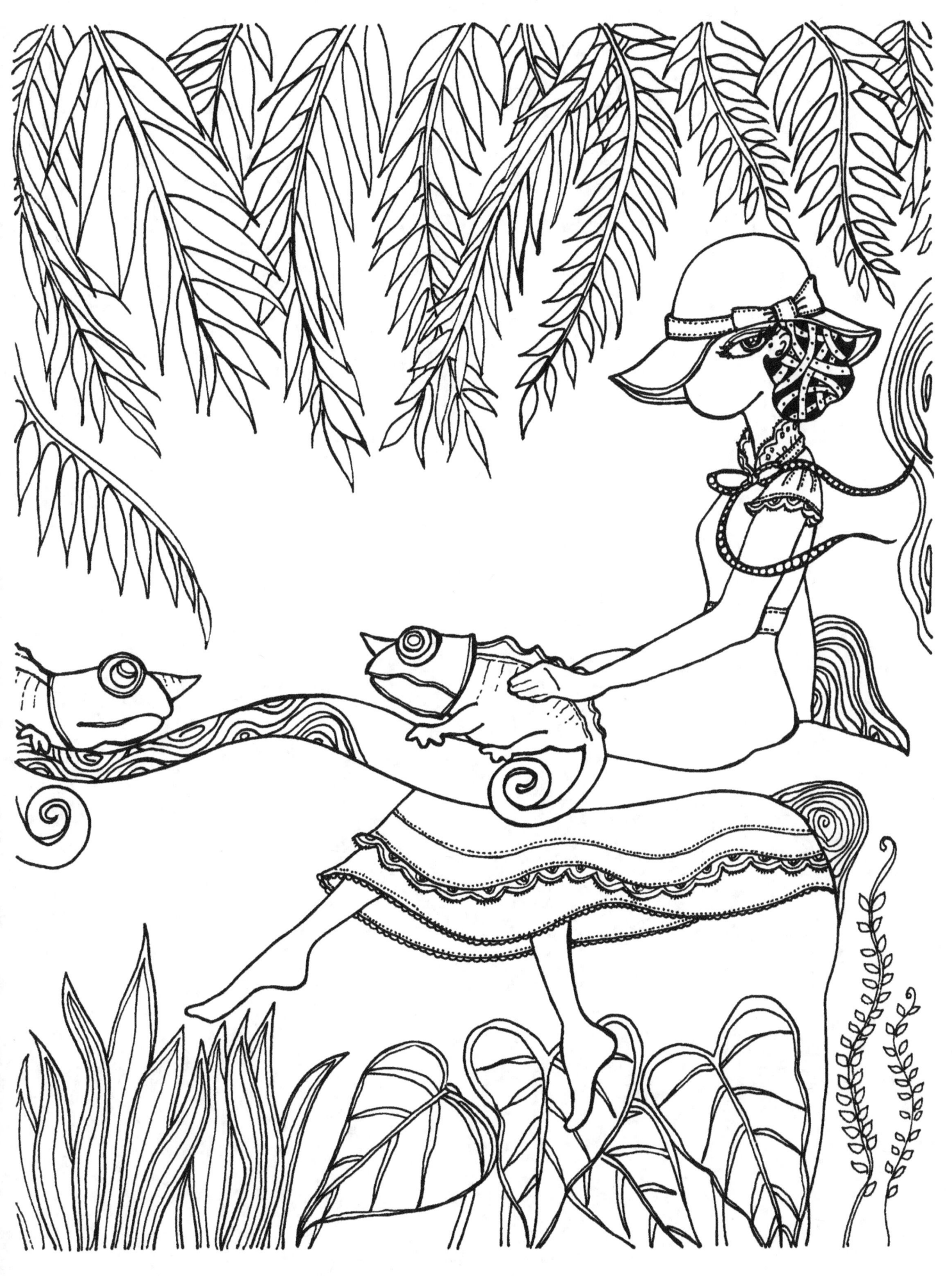

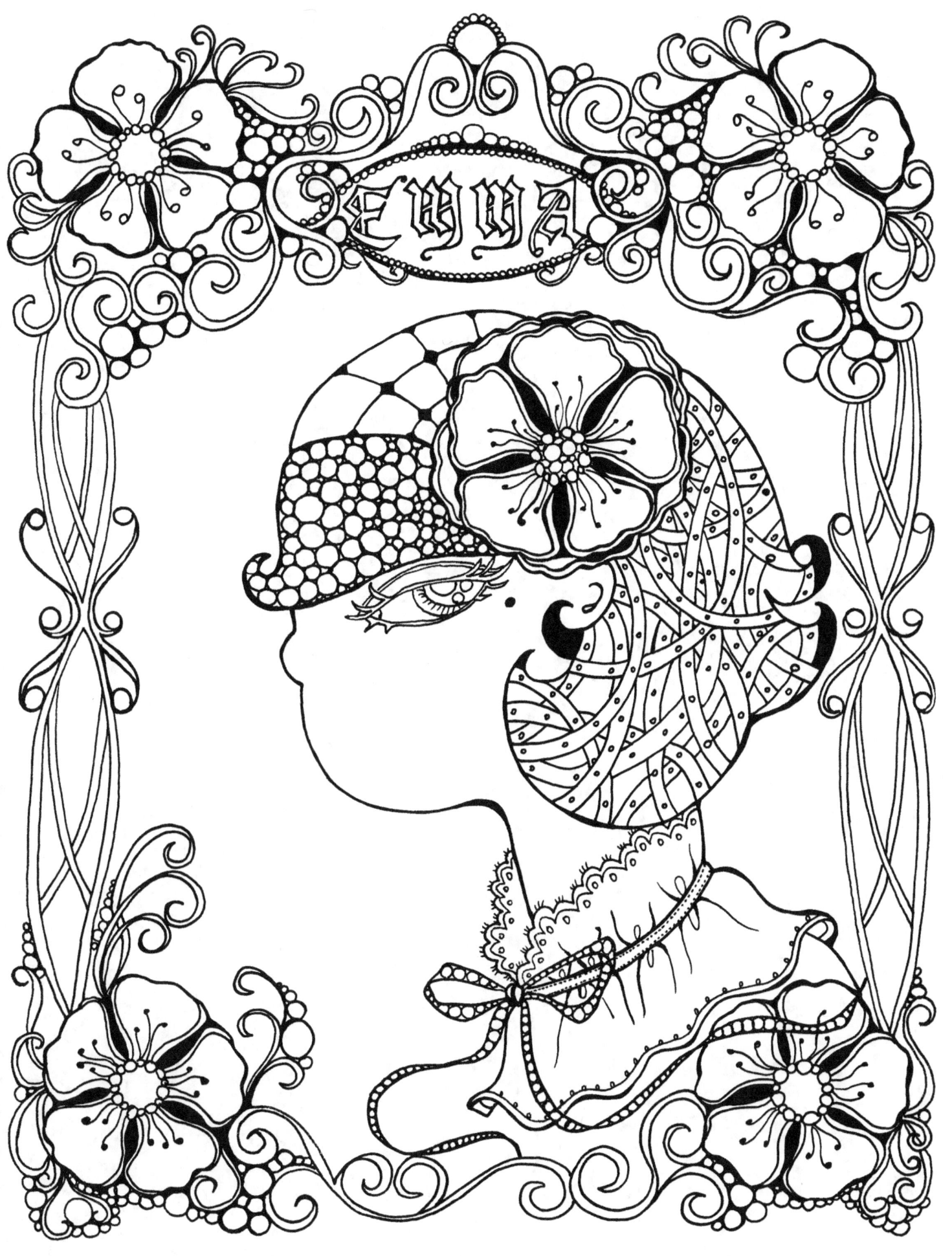

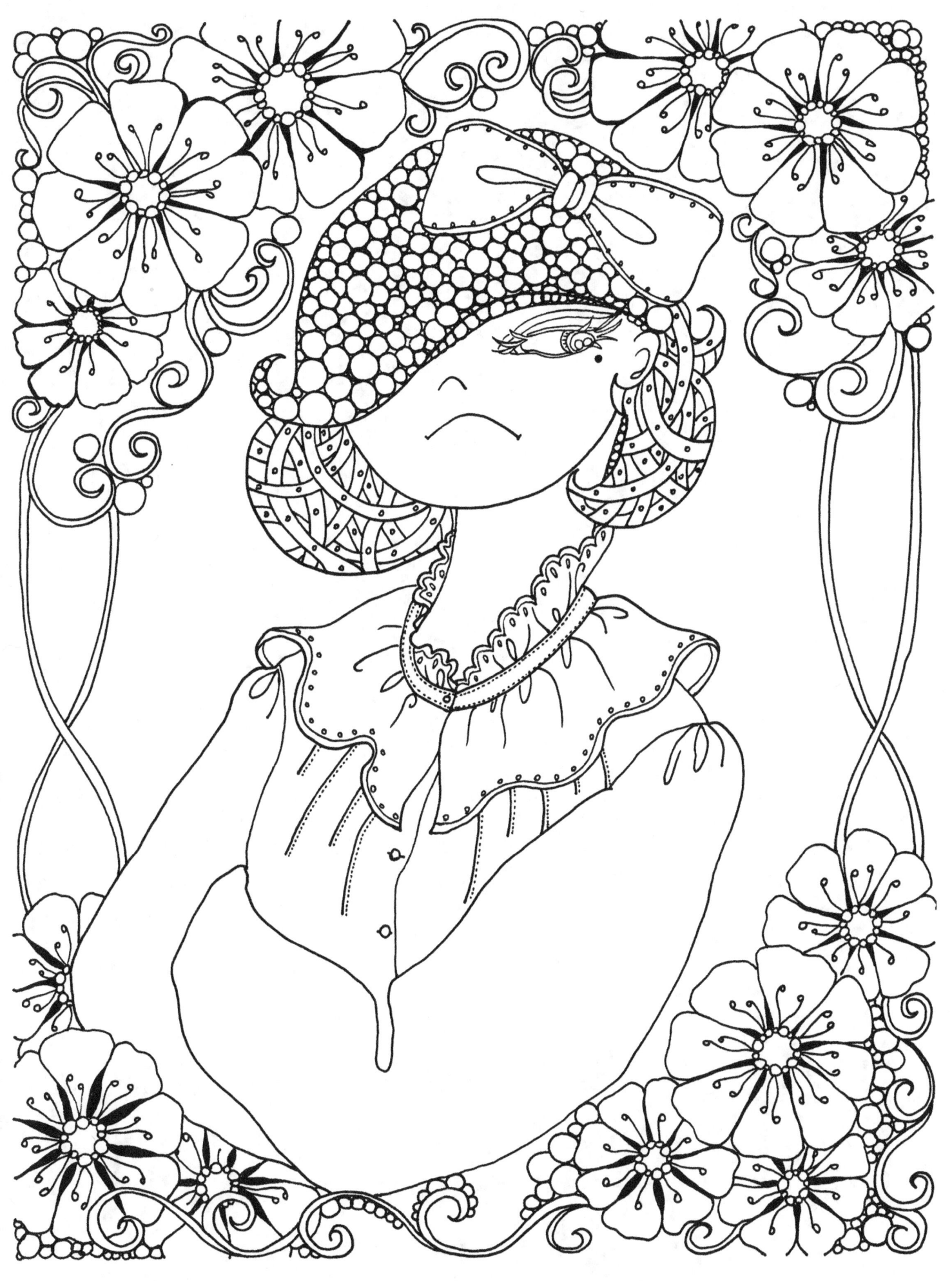

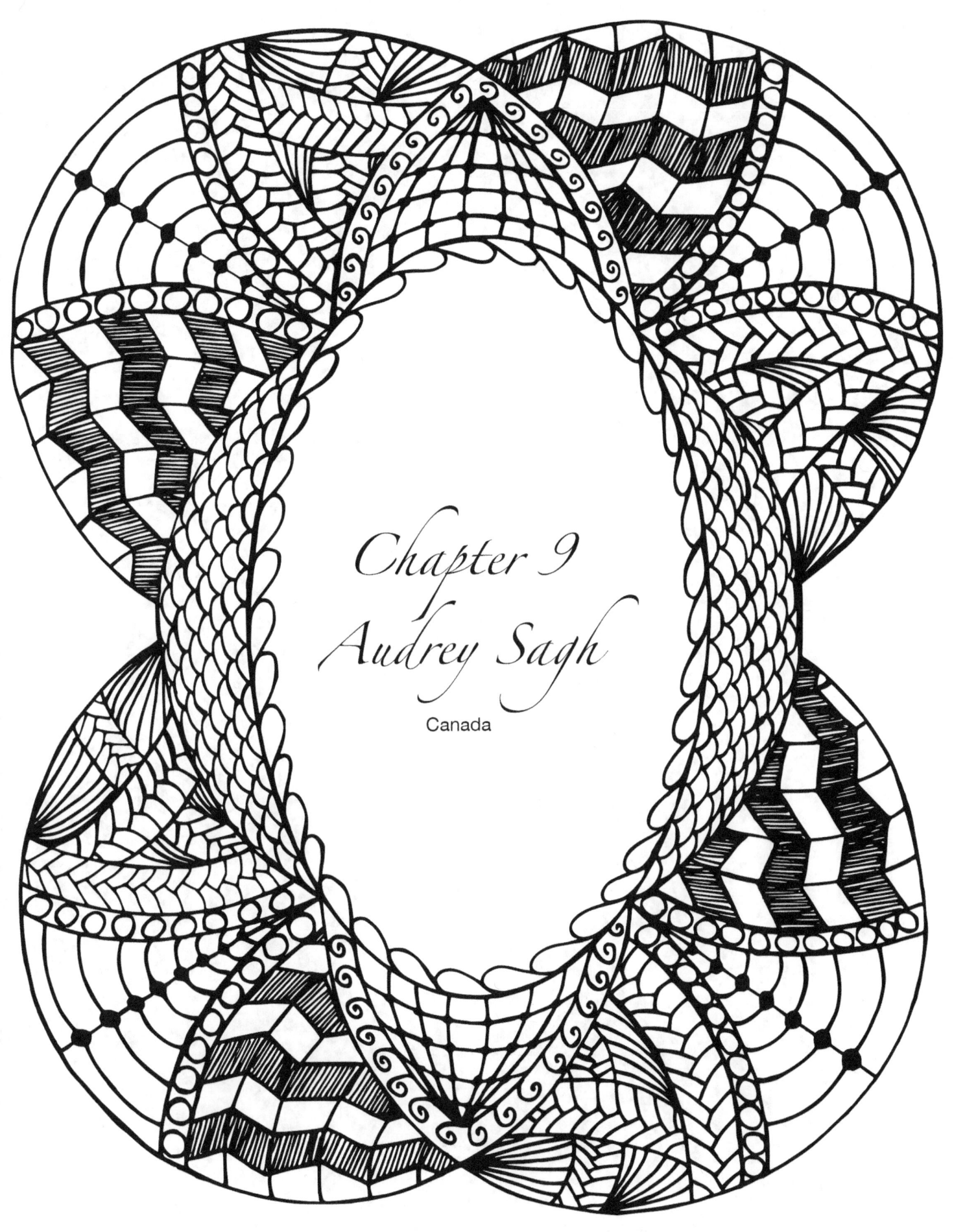

Chapter 9
Audrey Sagh

Canada

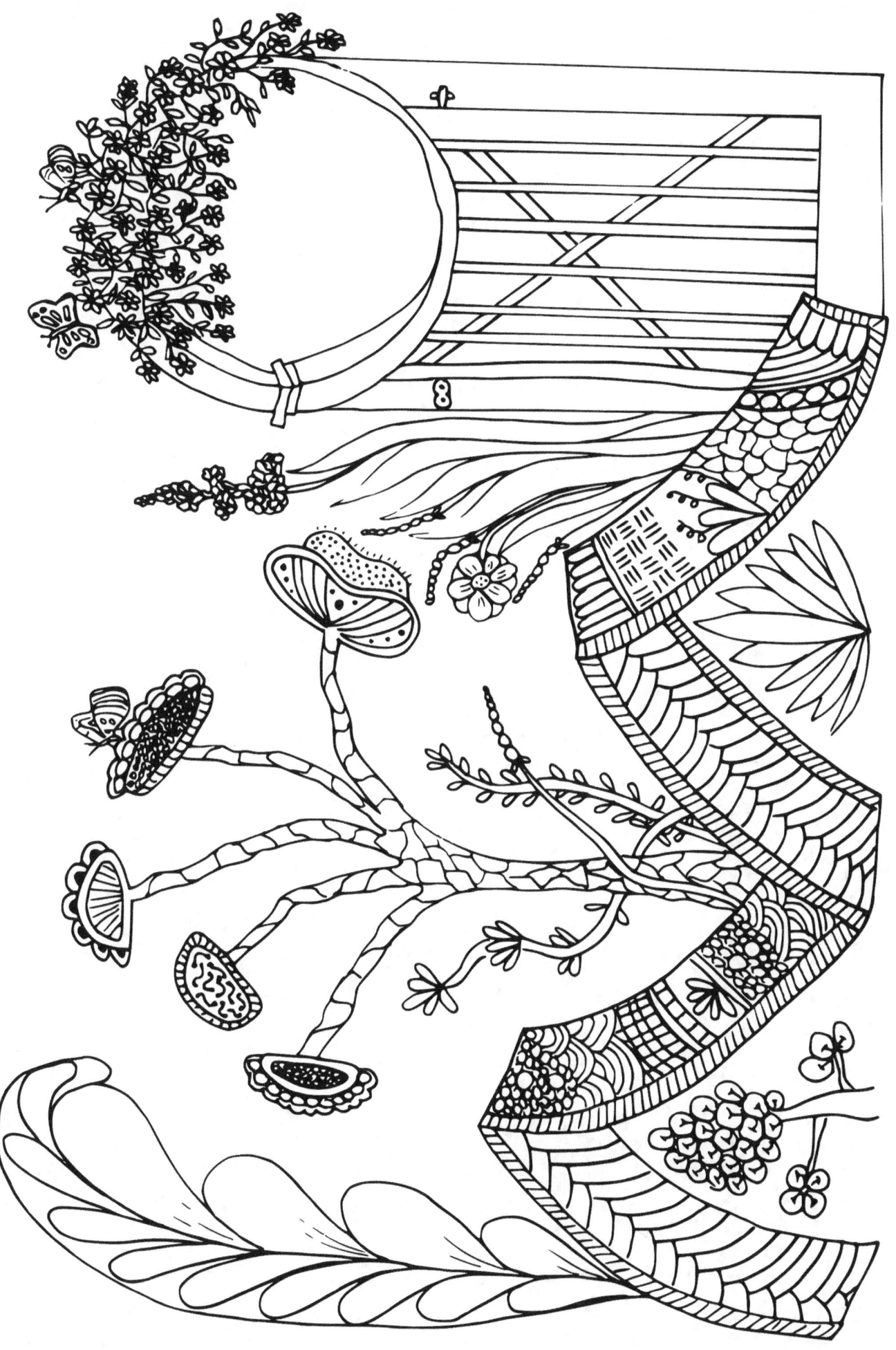

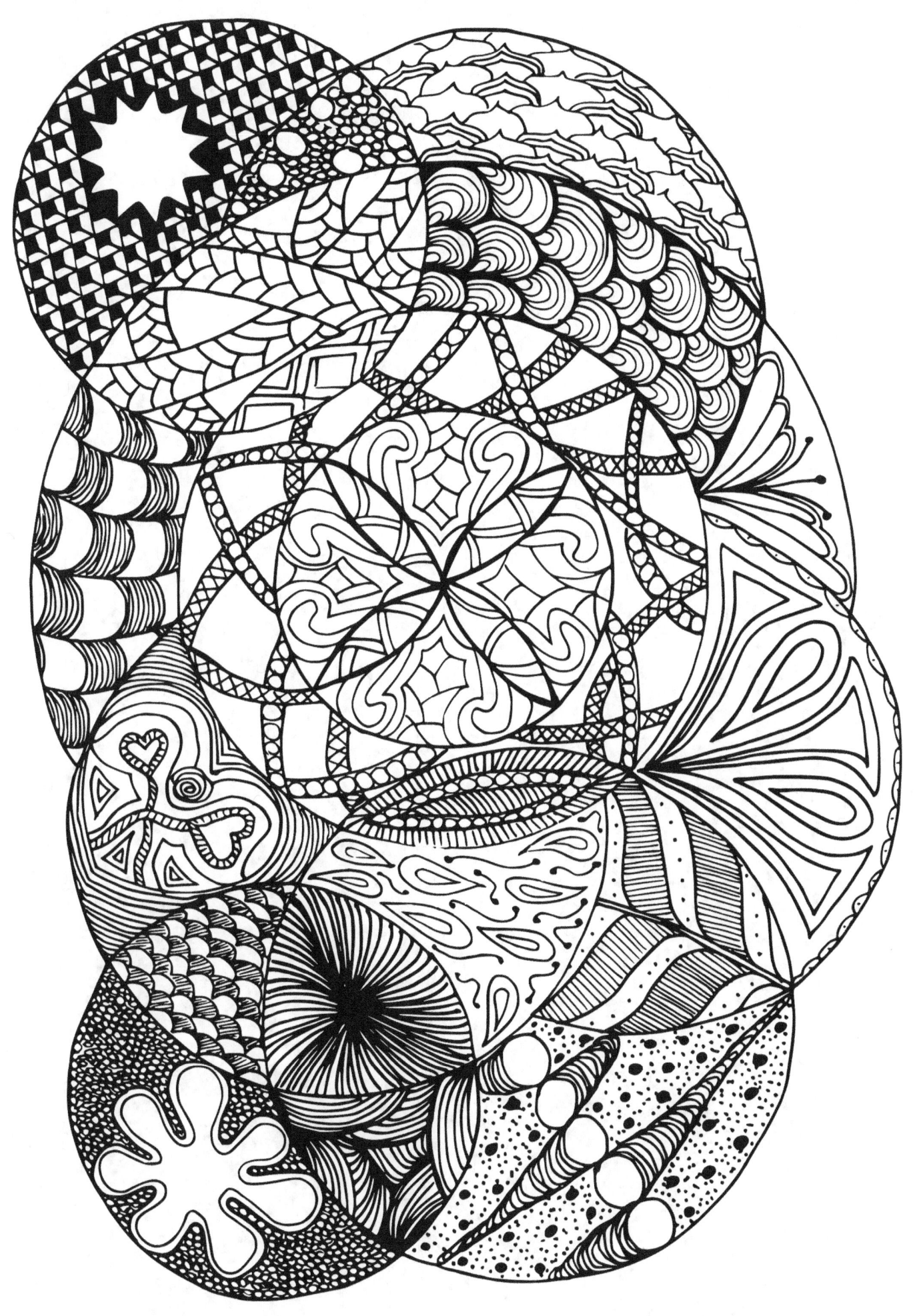

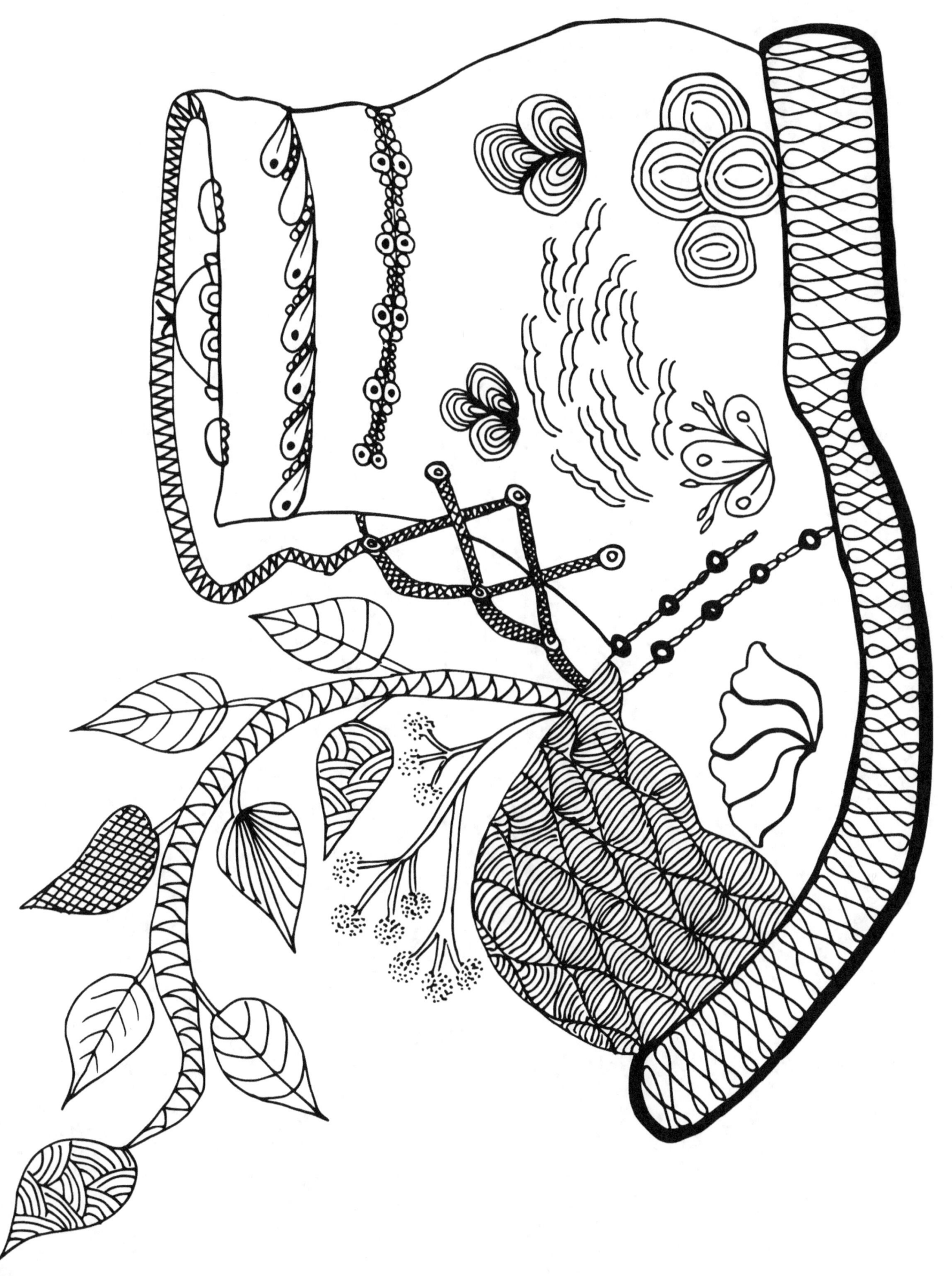

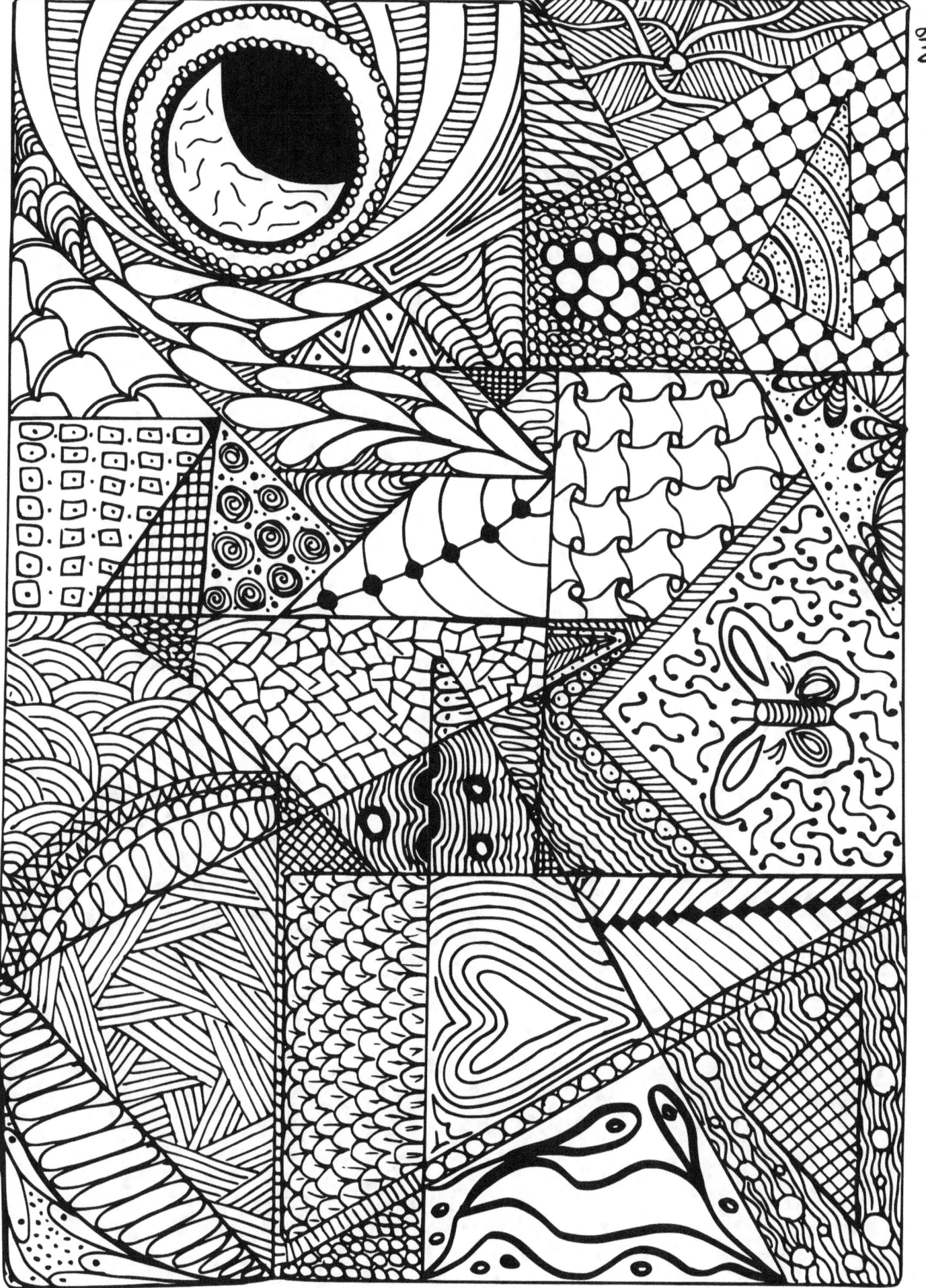

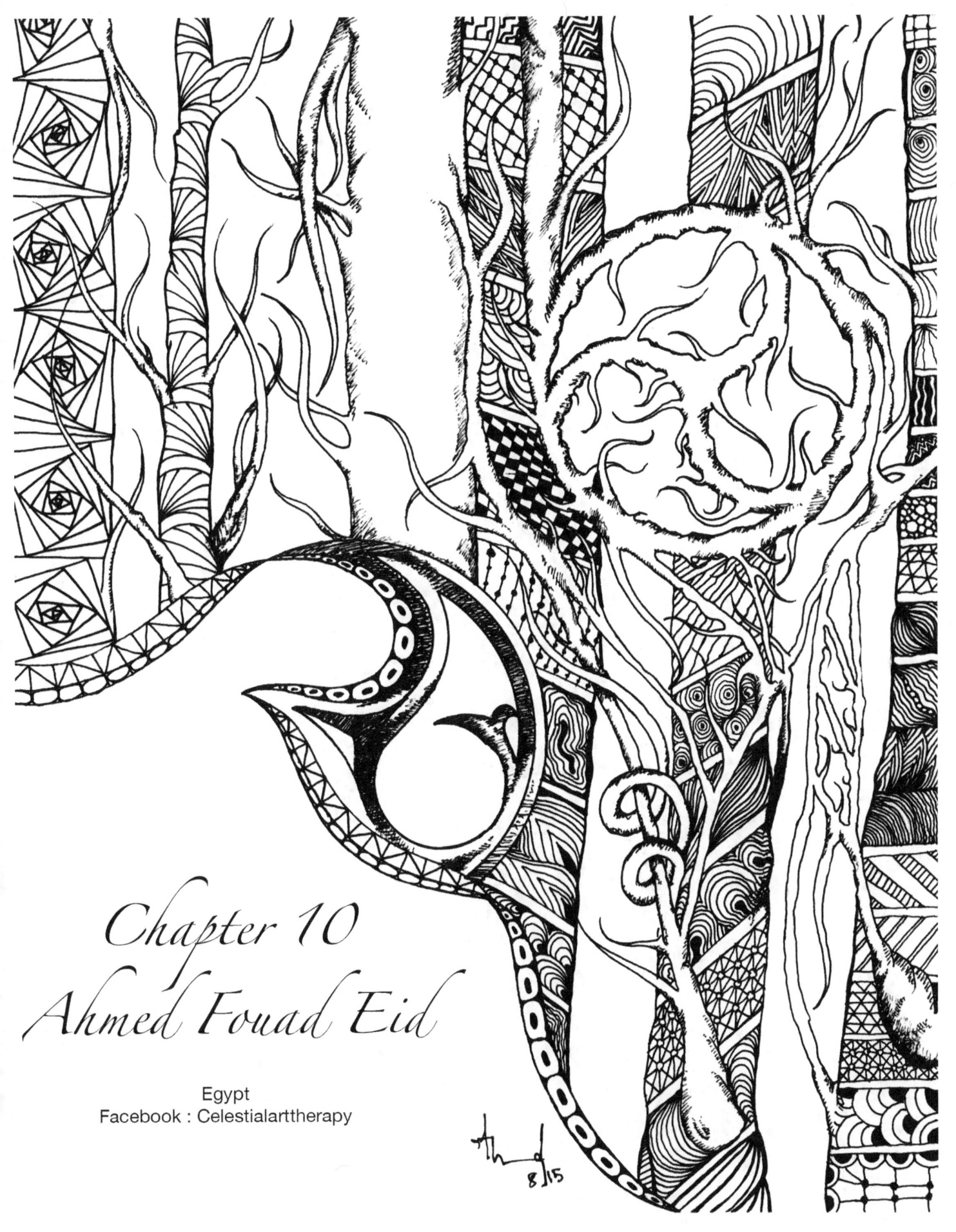

Chapter 10
Ahmed Fouad Eid

Egypt
Facebook : Celestialarttherapy

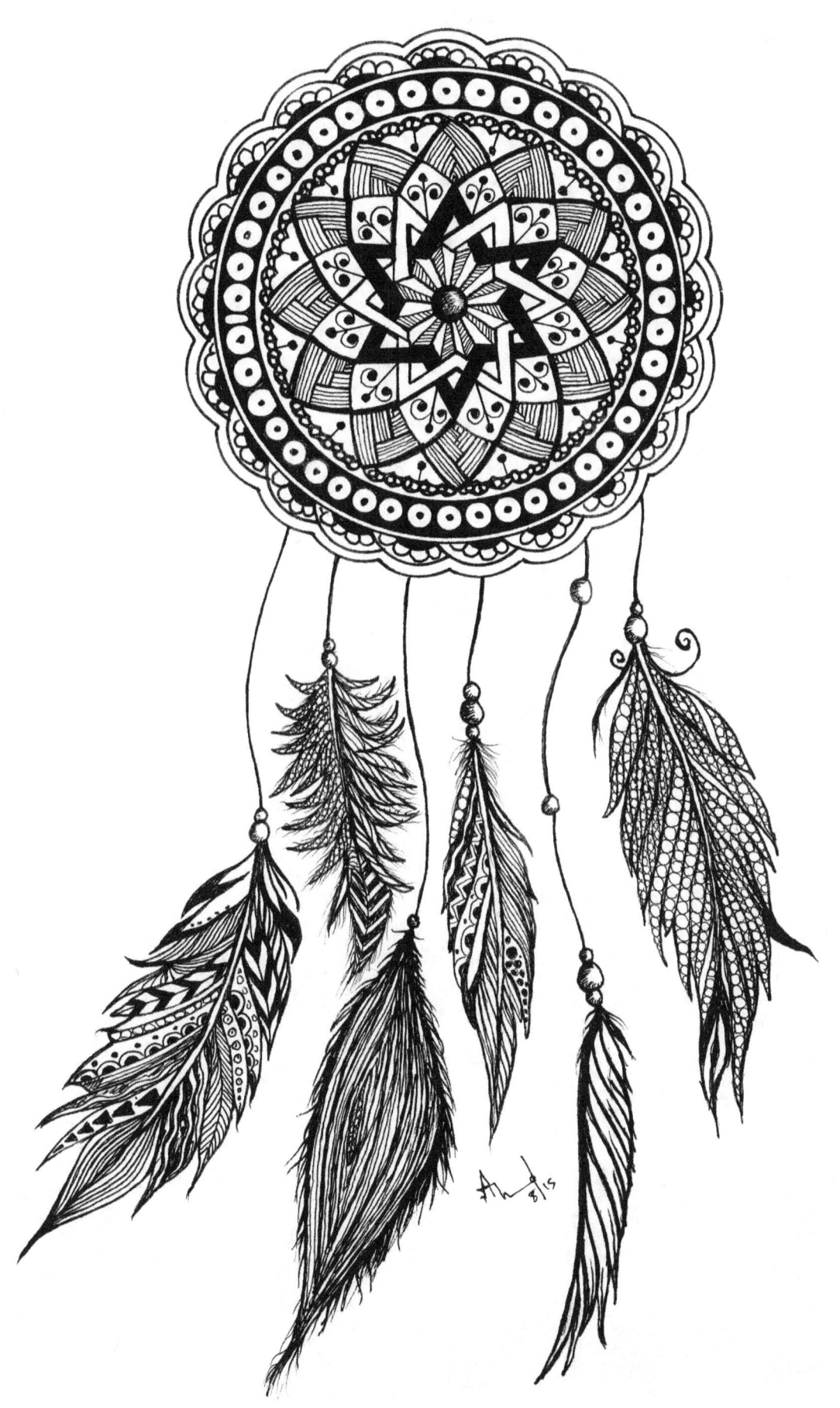

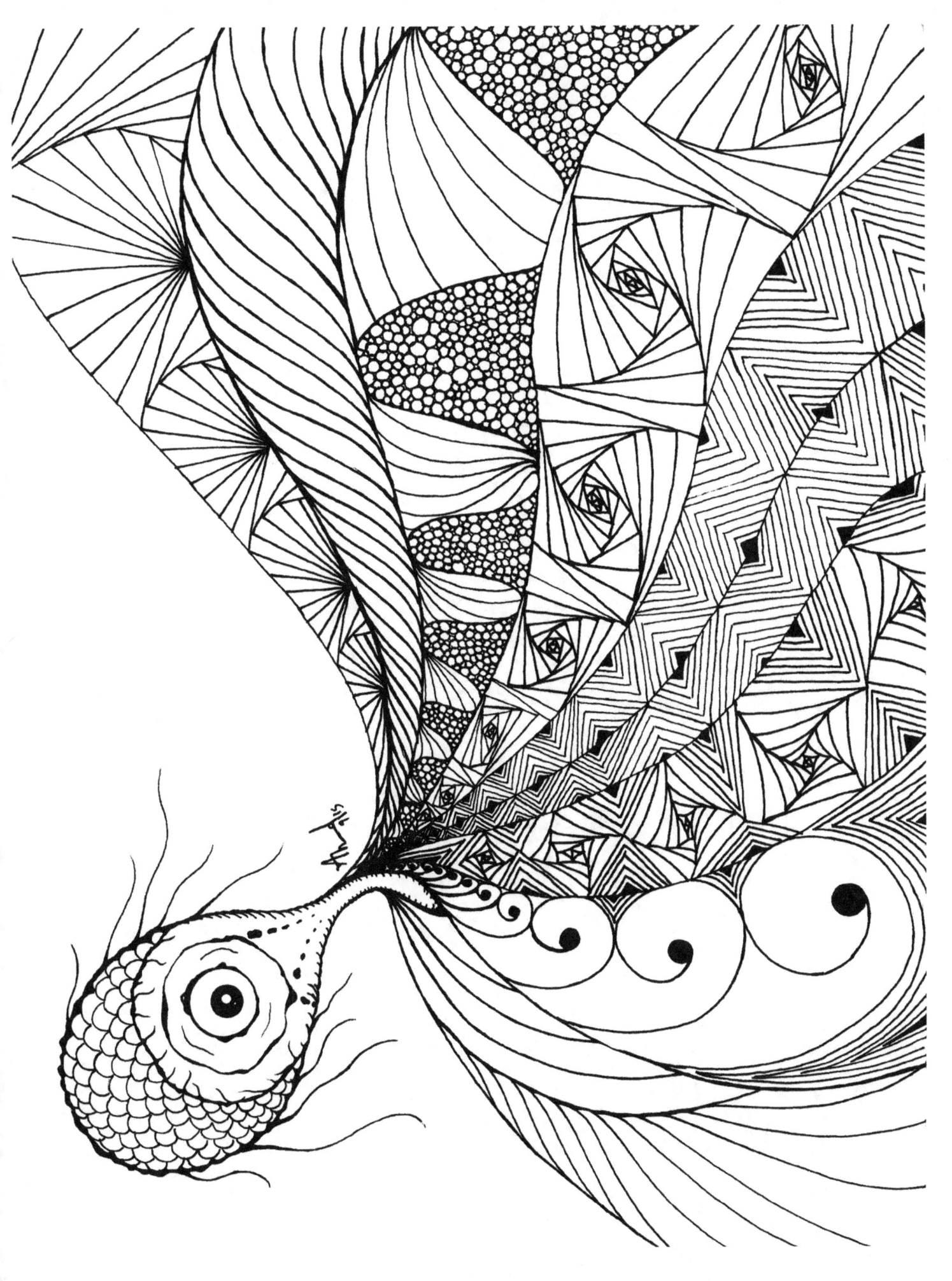

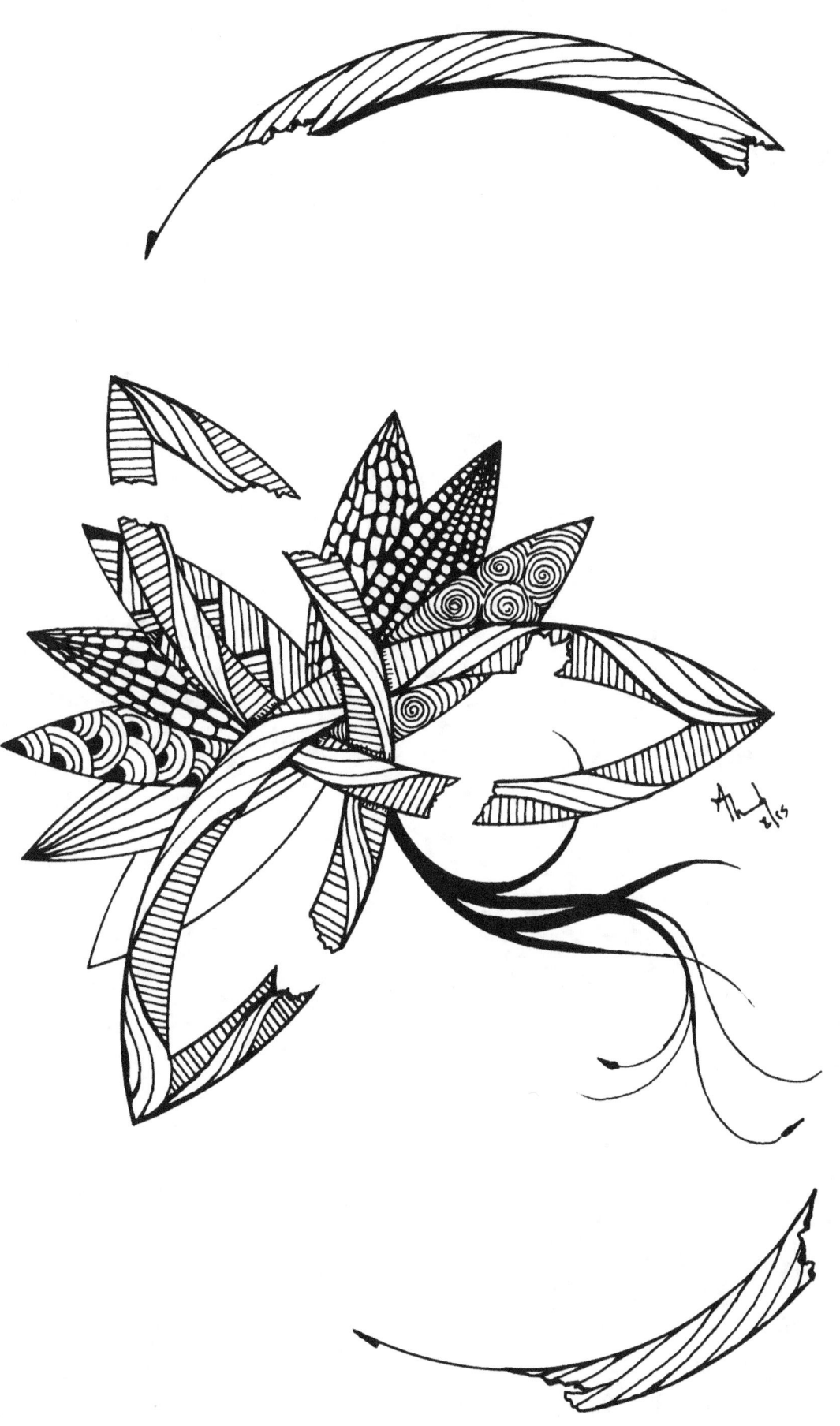

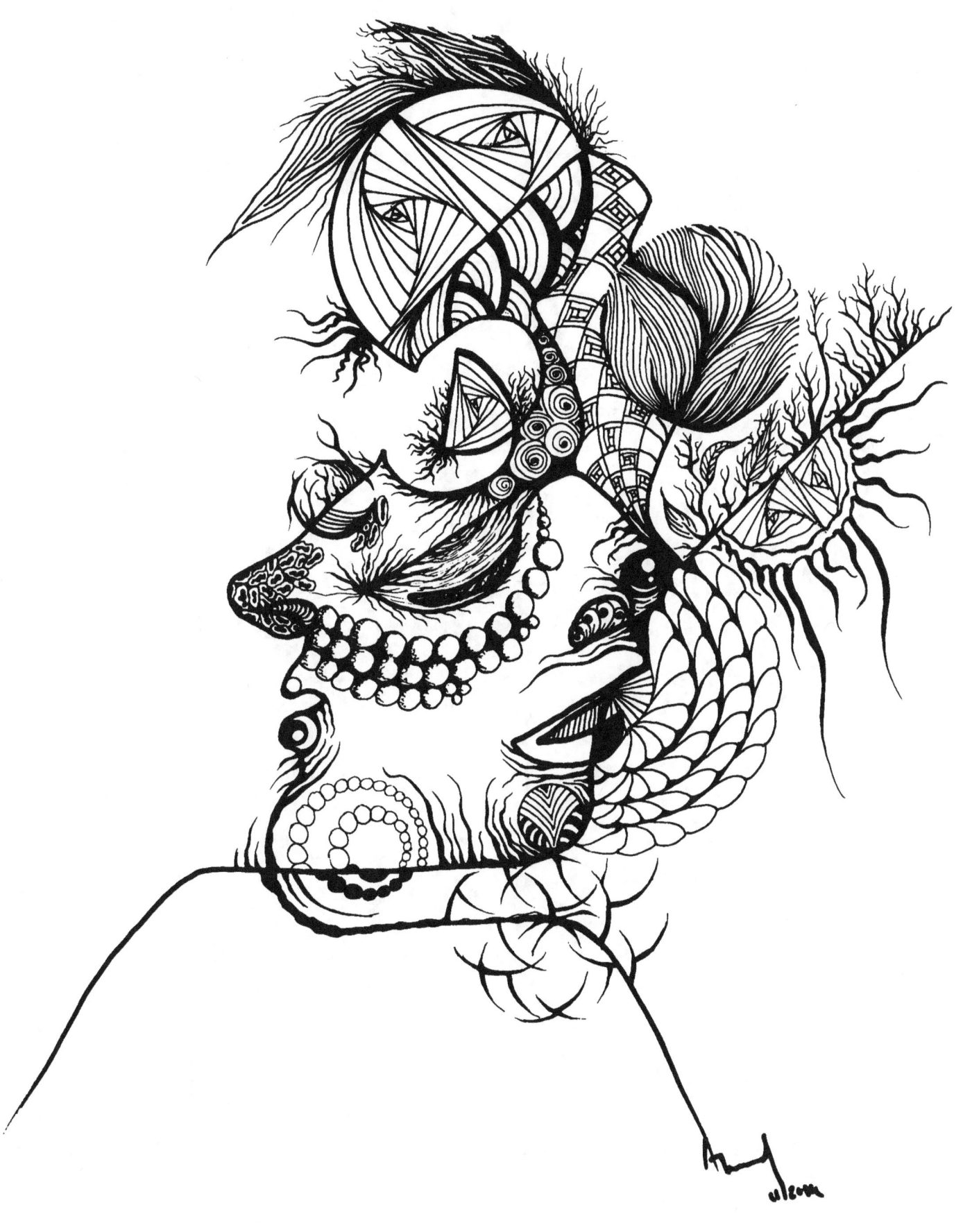

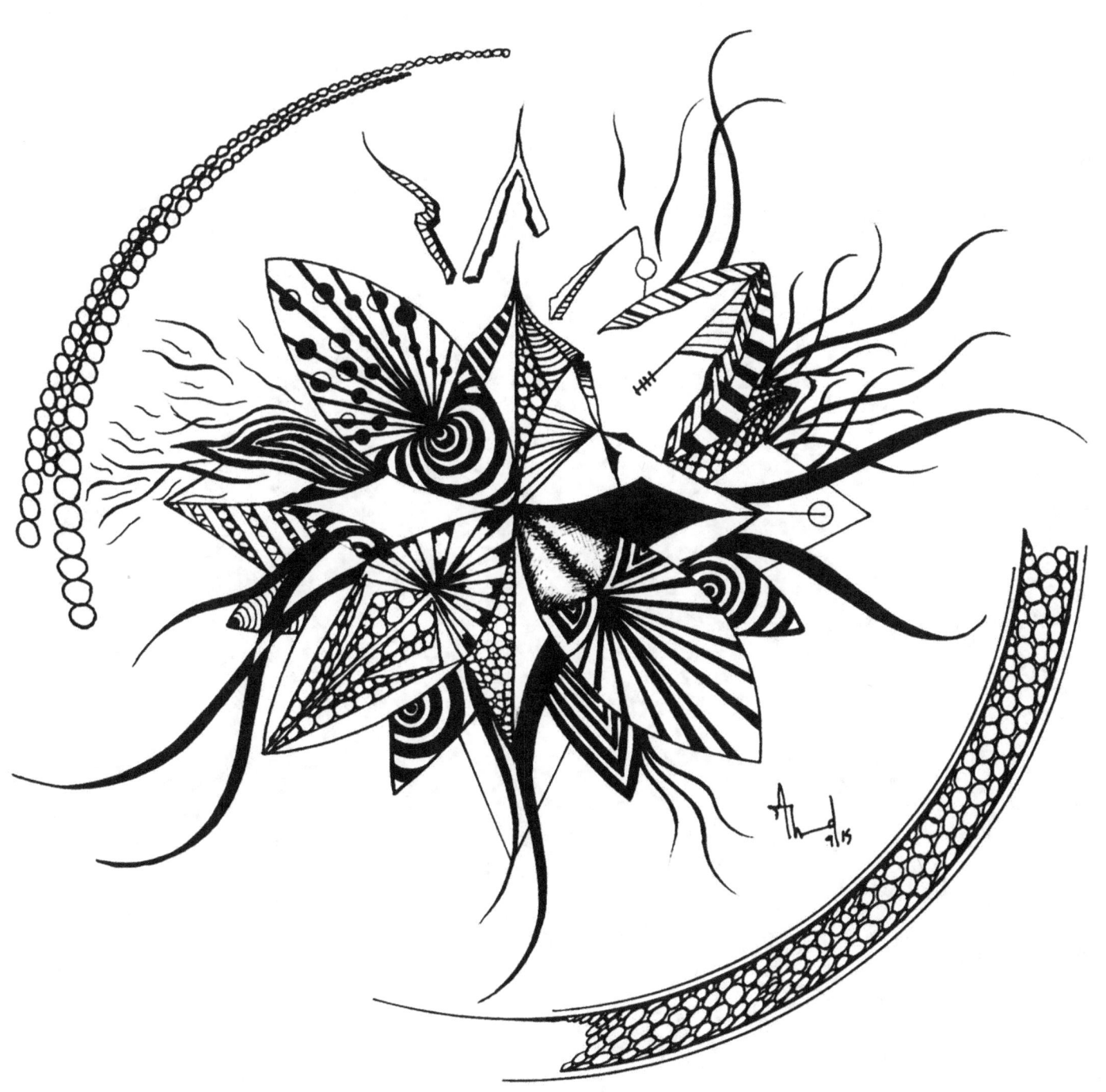

We from Global Doodle Gems, hope your journey through our book has been a pleasant one!

Please feel free to share your colored versions with us here:

https://www.facebook.com/groups/globaldoodlegems/

In our group you can meet the artists and enjoy exclusive freebies, video previews and participate in our and so much more...

if you are wishing, that you could have the Chapter pages without the text, well then swing on by the group and get them for free in the freebie pdf for volume 13.....

Are you curious about Volume 14?....well, just take a look at the next 2 pages and you will know what to exspect in the next volume of "Global Doodle Gems!

"Global Doodle Gems" Volume 14
Preview

Esther Lafiebre

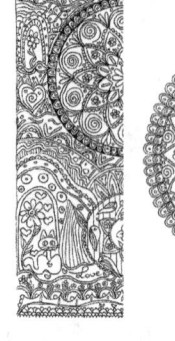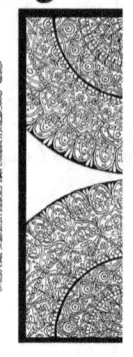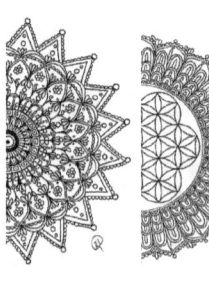

Les galaxies de 'Qi

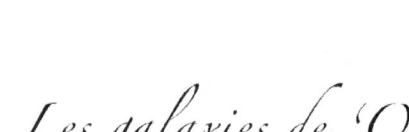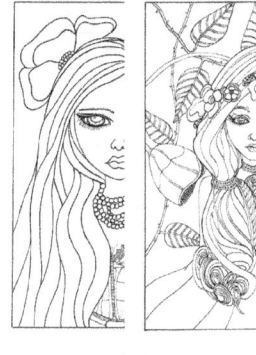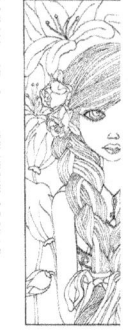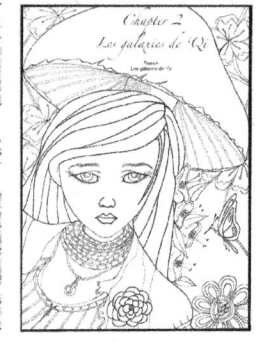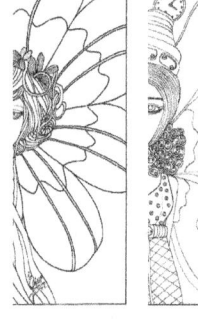

Marie-Eve Klein

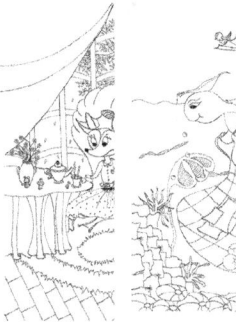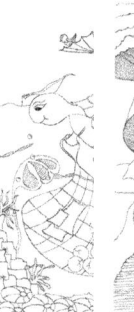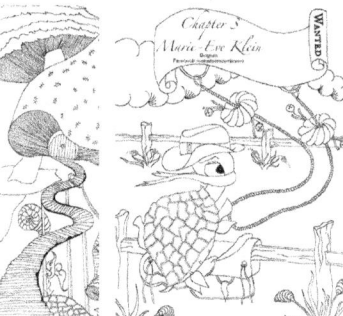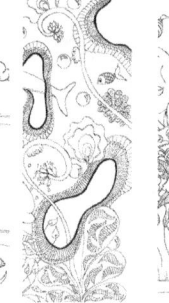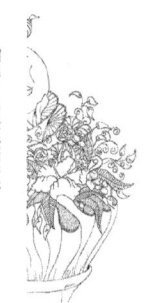

Jane Levi

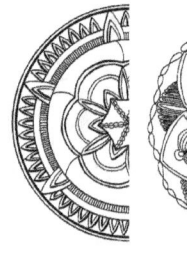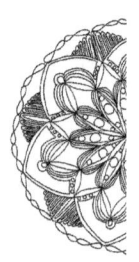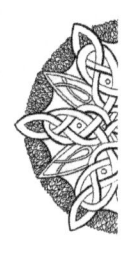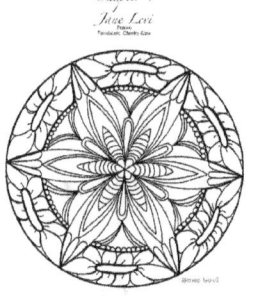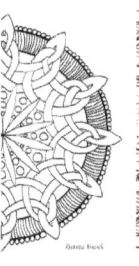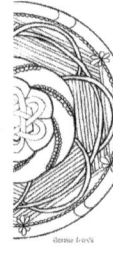

Irina Sergeeva

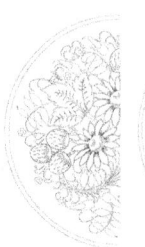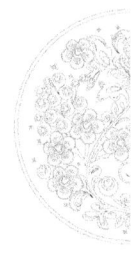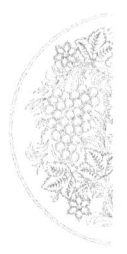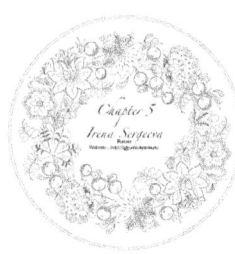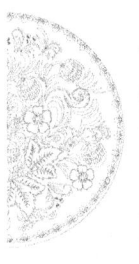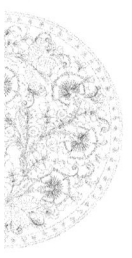

Joann Sands

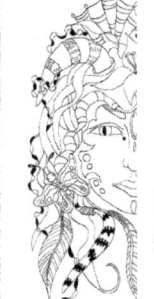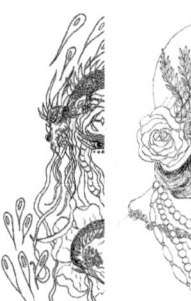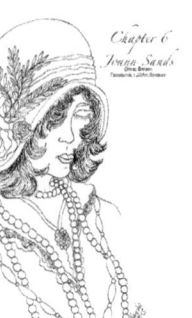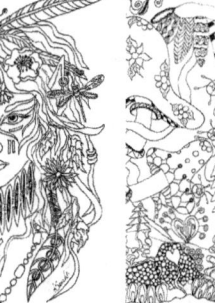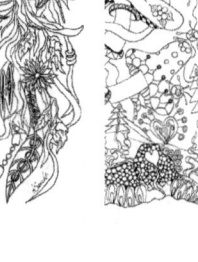

Fabienne Tosi

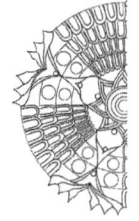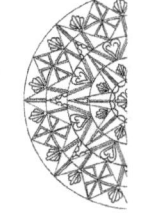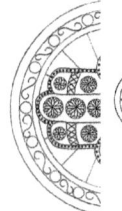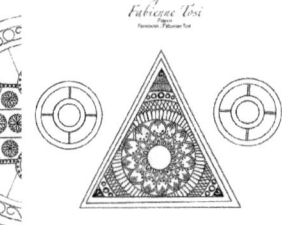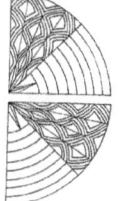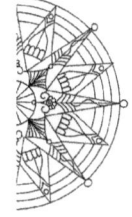

Asma Zergui

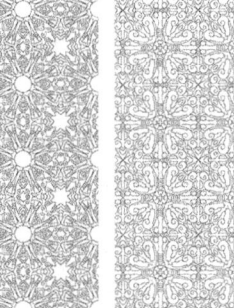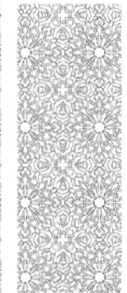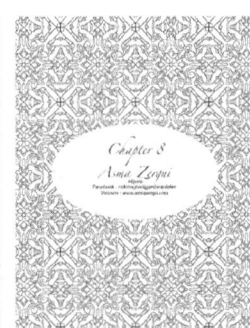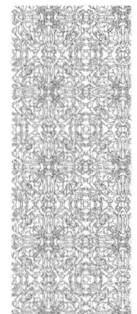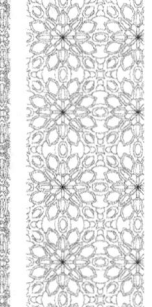

Mireille Westerduin,
Colour by Mi

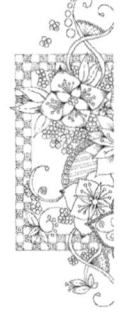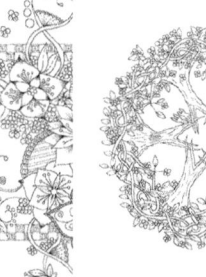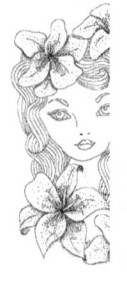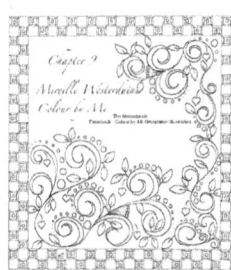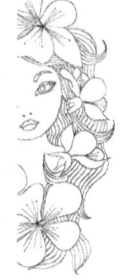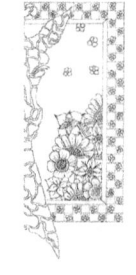

Maggie Lin

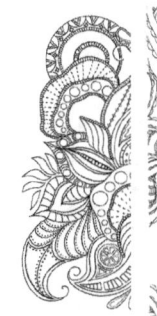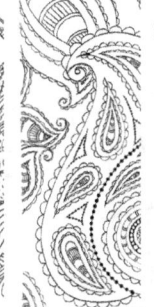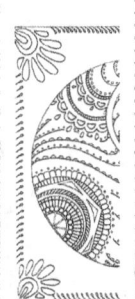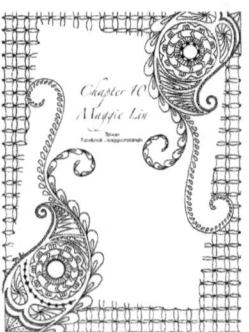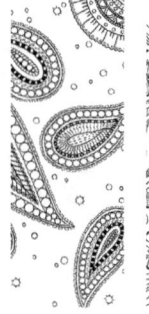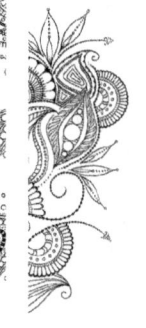

Meet the artists feautured in "GDG" Volume 14

Test Your Colors here ....
Charts from "My Pocket Color Companion"
and
"My Color Companion"

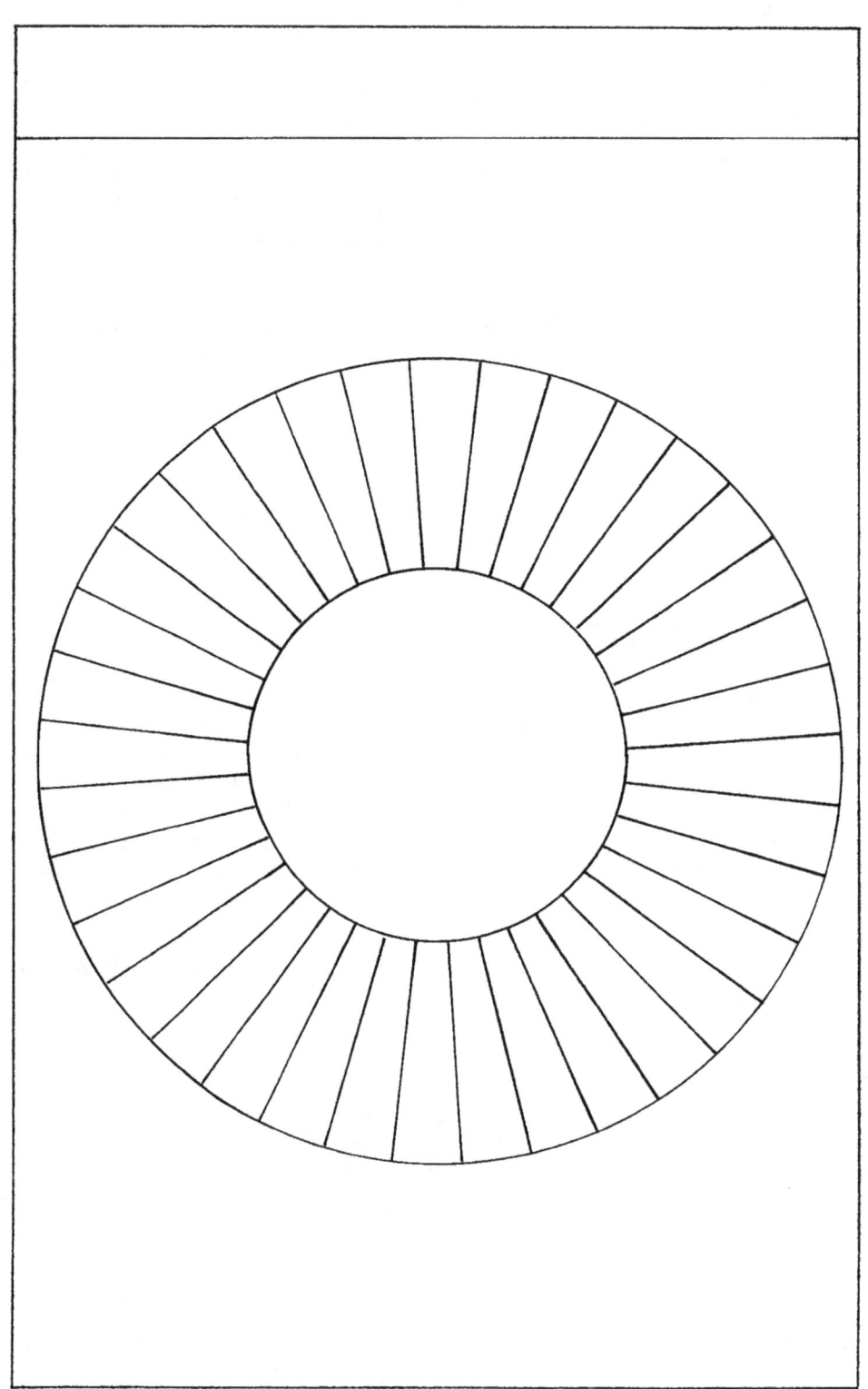

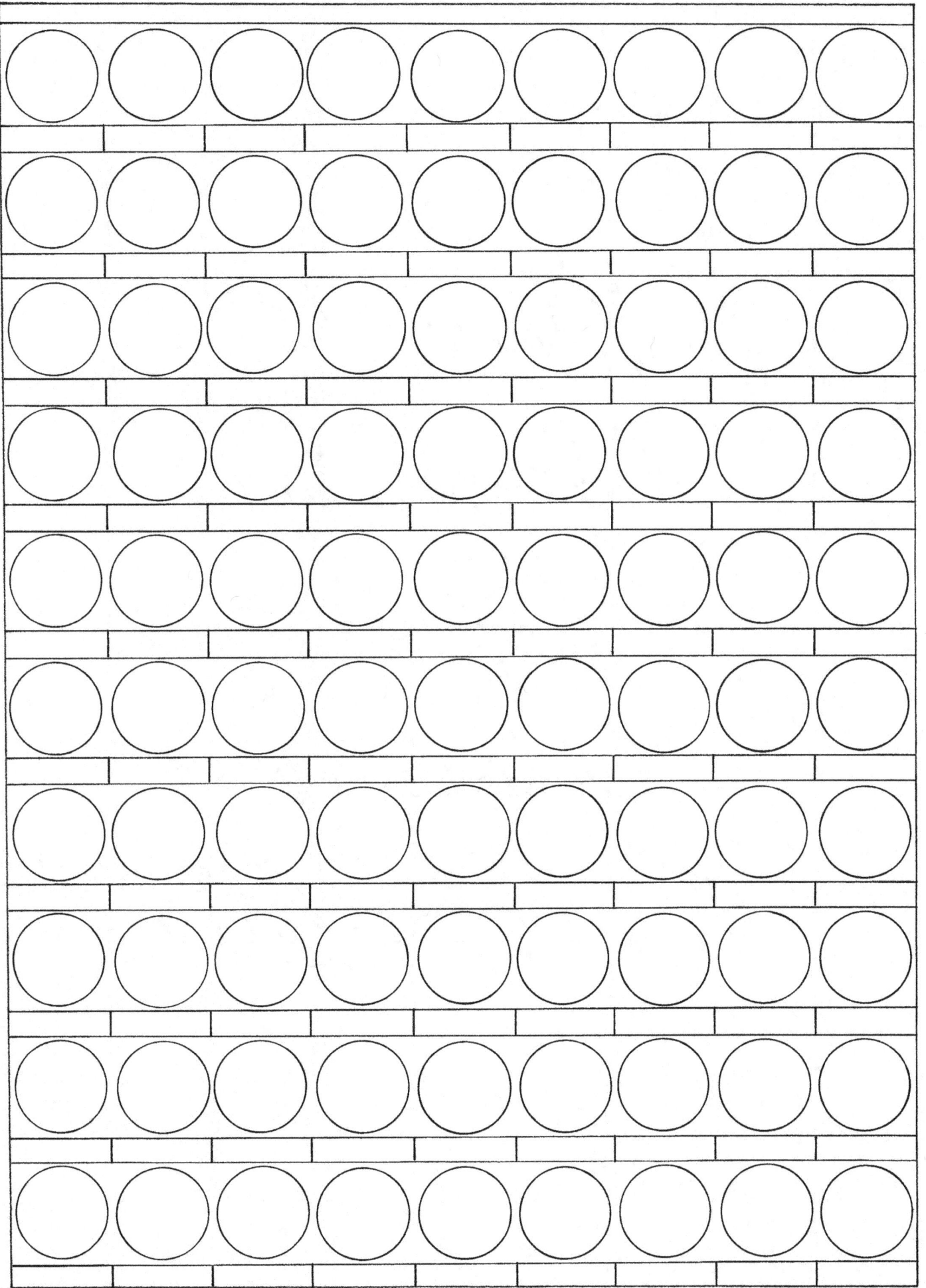

Published by
"GDG"
Global Doodle Gems

Global Doodle Gems Volume One
"The Ultimate International Coloring Book...an Epic Collection from Artists around the World"

Drawn by
Maggie Lin
&
Colored by
Laurence Roucou

www.ingramcontent.com/pod-product-compliance
Lightning Source LLC
Chambersburg PA
CBHW082207220526
45470CB00010B/3075